DESTINATION
GRAND CANYON

A view from the Grand Canyon's South Rim of the steep-walled abyss.

DESTINATION
GRAND CANYON

Photographs: Christian Heeb
Text: Helmut Friedrich

WINDSOR BOOKS
INTERNATIONAL

The Watchtower at Desert View, an impressive reproduction of an old Indian tower, provides an excellent view into the canyon.

CONTENTS

A view from the South Rim onto the Grand Canyon's deeply fissured and eroded terrain.

PANORAMA OF THE EARTH'S HISTORY: THE GRAND CANYON

There may be deeper and narrower ravines in the world, but no other is as magnificent, as awe-inspiring, fascinating and famous as the Grand Canyon.

A modern day traveller standing on the edge of this mighty cut in the earth's crust is somewhat prepared, for he has already seen numerous photographs and films or heard reports from others. And yet he still will be overwhelmed and amazed at how big, how dramatic the ravine is in actual fact. What could have gone through the minds of the first people to come here, the Indians, and what could have gone through the minds of the first Whites, who were totally unprepared when they reached the Grand Canyon?

Discovery and Exploration
of the Grand Canyon

Very little has been handed down to us on this subject. The Indians did not write, and the first Whites did not feel it was worthwhile to record their observations. It is conceivable, however, that the Indians, people for whom nature is especially sacred even today, venerated the Grand Canyon in their own way. The legends telling of its creation call the Grand Canyon by the name "Kaibab", which signifies a mountain standing on its head.

The first Europeans to see the canyon held very little sacred, and certainly not nature: they were gold-miners, and they were certainly not so much moved as alarmed, perplexed, disappointed and perhaps angered, when they stood on the edge of the Grand Canyon. They were members of the Coronado Expedition, a body of 336 Spaniards and one thousand Indians who set off through the American desert on their quest for the legendary Seven Gold Cities of Cibola, under the leadership of Francisco Vásquez de Coronado. They had heard from Indians living in this arid country of a great river somewhere to the north. Could the rich settlements be there? Coronado sent out a search party composed of twenty-five Spaniards led by Captain García López de Cárdenas, who reached the Grand Canyon, probably between today's Moran Point and

Desert View, after a journey of twenty-eight days. The men spent three days on the rim of the ravine without finding a way down into it. And consequently the quest for the golden cities failed.

After this vain attempt to get to know it, the canyon fell into oblivion. It was not visited again until two hundred years later, by Father Francisco Tomás Garcés of the San Xaver del Bac Spanish Mission near Tucson. He attempted to convert the Havasupai Indians living along the Colorado to Christianity. Although they welcomed him in a most friendly way and held a days-long feast, they still would not let themselves be converted. So this visit also failed, but at least the name Colorado was retained: the missionary was the first to report on the "Río Colorado", the red river.

In 1858, a fifteen metre (fifty foot) stern-wheeler, the "Explorer", progressed upriver from the Colorado estuary under the leadership of Lieutenant Joseph C. Ives, in an attempt to discover how far the Colorado was navigable. However, the journey ended shortly after the ship arrived close to today's Hoover Dam in the Black Canyon, which has since been flooded. The "Explorer" had run aground on hidden rocks. Some members of the crew were hurled overboard by the fierce impact and the ship was so heavily damaged that it was impossible to consider carrying on.

Ives and his men then tried to advance into the canyon on mules. But they soon encountered insurmountable obstacles and were forced to retrace their steps. Joseph C. Ives commented that they were the first group of Whites and would without doubt be the last to visit "this area devoid of all use. It appears to be Nature's intention to ensure that the Colorado, along with most of the isolated and majestic countryside, remains eternally unvisited and undisturbed." Since then, more than 100 million people have visited the Grand Canyon.

The interior of the canyon was not explored until 1869, when 35-year-old Major John Wesley Powell, who had lost an arm in the Civil War, made his legendary journey with his nine companions down the Colorado through the Grand Canyon, a journey fraught with losses and privation. The adventure which he and his men lived through,

A surprise for many visitors: the Grand Canyon is by no means a bleak, lifeless abyss. Each of the four climatic zones through which one passes on the descent into the canyon impresses by its individual and varied animal and plant life. This picture shows the colourful vegetation along Bright Angel Trail.

Along Bright Angel Trail: a cotton- wood tree, a type of poplar, provides shade…

the strain, hunger and fear of the next rapids was recorded in Major Powell's diary, "Exploration of the Colorado River of the West and its Tributaries". Four simple wooden boats were launched on 24 May 1869, in Green River Station, Wyoming, a town on the Green River, the largest tributary of the Colorado, and attainable by railway. Only two boats and six half-starved men arrived at their destination on 29 August. Eight hundred river kilometres (five hundred miles) lay behind them. One participant gave up after six weeks, whilst still on the Green River. Three others who no longer wished to expose themselves to the strain of the rapids broke off from the expedition on 28 August, one day before the two remaining boats reached calm waters; the three were killed by Indians, who mistakenly believed them to be guilty of a crime committed by other Whites.

The Colorado River – The River in the Desert

The Grand Canyon and the Colorado River are inseparably joined. It is therefore best to learn a little more about this river. Along with its larger tributaries (the Green, San Juan, Dolores, Little Colorado, Gunnison, and Virgin Rivers), as well as approximately one hundred additional medium and smaller rivers (such as the Paria, Escalante and Dirty Devil Rivers) from which water flows only periodically,

the Colorado forms one of the largest river systems in North America. It drains an area of 632,000 square kilometres (245,000 square miles), entirely or partially in- cluding seven American states: Arizona, California, Col- orado, New Mexico, Nevada, Utah and Wyoming. This is an area equal to one-twelfth of the USA and almost double the area of the Federal Republic of Germany.

From its source in the Rocky Mountains at an altitude of 3,184 metres (10,444 feet), the Colorado follows a 2,335 kilometre-long (1,450 mile-long) path to the Gulf of California; of this, approximately 1,600 kilometres (1,000 miles) flows through nineteen relatively deep canyons, such as Cataract Canyon, Westwater Canyon, Glen Canyon (known today as Lake Powell) and, last but not least, the Grand Canyon, until joining Lake Mead. During its course, it changes from a crystal clear mountain river (formerly laden with red-brown sediment) to a sweeping and roar- ing river, ending as a murky, salt rivulet before entering the gulf. Before Glen Canyon Dam was built, the Colorado carried up to 8,500,000 litres (1,870,000 Imperial gallons) of water per second and attained speeds of up to 20 kilometres (12.5 miles) per hour. These numbers illus- trate that it is amongst the great rivers of the world.

The Colorado was the undisputed "world champion" for the transportation of material, until the Glen Canyon

…and a smoke tree (Psorothamnus spinosus), a member of the pulse family.

Dam was built. On 13 September 1927 it conveyed in a 24-hour period twenty-seven million tons of sludge! The pebbles which the unleashed river pushed ahead of it on this day are not included in these calculations; it has been estimated that the amounts were equivalent to the amount of sludge conveyed.

At first glance it seems amazing that the entire Colorado area and its tributaries are (or were) a desert, formerly called the Great American Desert by government officials and cartographers when first confronted with the region following the Lousiana Purchase land acquisition. A gigantic river system with many branches in the desert! This appears paradoxical. But when one considers that this desert is a stone desert in which rivers have cut deep grooves over millions of years through the continuous lift of the Colorado Plateau and its peripheral areas and hence, contrary to the Nile, for example, can not irrigate the embankment areas; and if one considers further that today the Colorado and its tributaries owe their waters to the snows and thunderstorms of the Rocky Mountains, then the apparent contradiction is clarified.

The Rocky Mountains are the most important water source of the Colorado. This explains the uneven course of its stream bed: sparse in winter, swollen during the spring thaw and somewhat calmer again in autumn.

The Taming of a River

The abundance of water in the Colorado and its gradient, as well as the dry desert terrain through which it flows, soon led to the consideration of how its water-power could benefit mankind.

The Colorado was used for profit as early as the turn of the century. At that time, land surveyors noticed that the Imperial Valley in southern California was 72 metres (235 feet) below sea-level. It was not very costly to divert water for irrigation purposes from the Colorado through a canal into this hollow. The canal was begun in 1901, and two years later it was already possible to cultivate the newly irrigated land.

However, shortly after this, in 1905, the inlet locks of the canal were destroyed during a flooding of the Colorado: the river poured over the canal edges and flooded the Imperial Valley. It formed a lake the size of which continuously increased, also causing the recently built Southern Pacific Railroad to flood. In just fifteen days, workers were able to seal the Colorado's breakthrough with rocks from hundreds of freight trains, forcing the river back into its old bed. The 56 kilometre- (35 mile-) long Salton Lake remained behind, between the Imperial and the Coachella Valleys, with a higher salt content than the Pacific.

This somewhat temporary action was followed in 1922 by a professional "taming". At that time, those states bordering on the Colorado River concluded the Colorado River Compact, the first contract in history which covers the multiple uses of a river system: irrigation, flood control, energy and tourism. Pride can be taken in the achievements attained to date: all told, a total of nine dams regulate the course of the Colorado and its tributaries, and ensures water distribution and energy extraction. In addition, the Colorado has become the most intensively used river in the world.

In place of the dramatic early merging with the Gulf of California, as described by Joseph C. Ives in 1858 ("The wide surface of the river around us boiled and foamed like water in a kettle. And then, after a short while, the whole thing returned – with the thundering of a cataract"), only black-brown murky salt water trickles into the Gulf, no longer Colorado water, just sewage. The Colorado has been tamed; the former bronco, the tempestuous wild horse, is today just a tired farm horse. But according to estimates, its usefulness for agriculture, energy production and recreation is to be assessed at more than one billion dollars per year.

As a result of the regulation of the Colorado's flow, three harvests per annum are possible in former desert areas of California and Arizona; oranges, apricots, strawberries, peaches and almonds flourish in abundance, and in addition to this, the great artificial lakes - Lake Powell, Lake Mead and Lake Havasu - offer millions of holiday-makers excellent facilities for water sports.

The Use of Water-Power

The first step towards using the Colorado on a large scale began with the Boulder Canyon Project Act. The construction of the Boulder Dam was determined by the law of 1928. This dam, which was erected between 1930 and 1936 and which is a masterpiece of American civil engineering, is still, at 221 metres (725 feet), one of the highest dams in the world. It was renamed Hoover Dam in honour of a former American President, Herbert C. Hoover, in 1947. Lake Mead, which was formed as a result of this dam, has a surface of 593 square kilometres (230 square miles) and a capacity of 38.5 billion cubic metres (50 billion cubic yards); it is consequently one of the largest artificial lakes in the United States. In surface, it takes a close second place only to Lake Powell (660 square kilometres/255 square miles).

No artificial lake in the world is everlasting, not so much because the cement of the dam crumbles with time, or that it is washed away by floods due to insufficient mooring in the surrounding rocks, as has happened on occasion. No, the major cause for the limited lifetime of an artificial lake

is the sediment, the not insignificant particles of matter carried in by the dammed-up river, which build up over long periods of time.

There has been some talk that this problem applies to the Colorado in particular. The river conveys approximately 400,000 tons of sediment daily and probably an equivalent amount as pebbles on the river-bed. With such an amount of material influx, the 38.5 billion cubic metres (50 billion cubic yards) of water in Lake Mead would be replaced in only three hundred-thirty years; the lake simply would be "full". But this calculation is too pessimistic, for the amount of pebbles cannot be measured accurately, and, in addition, up to twenty percent of the suspended matter flows through the turbines at the foot of the dam, creating another artificial lake. More optimistically estimated, Lake Mead's lifetime should be at least another five hundred years.

But it will exist for much longer: in 1956 construction began on Glen Canyon Dam above Hoover Dam, a few kilometres north of Lee's Ferry. Construction of the Lake Powell Dam, named after the explorer, was completed seven years later. This lake is now the catchment area of the material carried by the Colorado. It takes on the majority (320,000 tons) of the 400,000 above-mentioned tons of sludge per year, as well as all the pebbles. Only "new" pebbles from the Grand Canyon and its side canyons are pushed into Lake Mead today.

Due to the construction of Glen Canyon Dam, Lake Mead will exist at least five times longer than estimated above. However, Lake Powell will only be around for five hundred to one thousand years. This "exchange", bound up with the sacrifice of Glen Canyon (more about this later), is incomprehensible and unforgivable in the minds of many conservationists.

Some water management experts also consider Lake Powell a mistake, for, in the dry desert region through which the Colorado flows, artificial lakes are very problematic: typically, the Arizona desert has an annual precipitation of only two hundred millimetres (eight inches) and an evaporation rate calculated to be ten times greater than that. Some 2.5 cubic kilometres (0.37 cubic miles) of water are lost each year through evaporation of the artificial lakes; this amount was not taken into consideration when the contract was officially concluded in 1922.

In the eyes of the conservationists, this error, discovered too late, also has a good side: the mere existence of this mistake prohibits the construction of additional artificial lakes, for their possible use is cancelled out by the additional evaporation. Consequently, the thoughtless plan to dam the river again with the Bridge Canyon Dam, and consequently to flood the Grand Canyon, will remain forever in the planners' files.

The canyon's rock formations are the result of the different forces of erosion: the growth of lichen and other plants, downpours and storms, extreme temperature swings and the blasting power of water and ice. A view from Mather Point on the South Rim.

A Natural Wonder is Flooded

"The nation's playground", "a great place of fun", deep blue water, 3,140 kilometres (1,950 miles) of shoreline (twice as much as the West Coast of the USA without Alaska), a natural wonder par excellence: this is what Lake Powell is to some; to others, it is an unforgivable offence against nature in one of its most beautiful locations, the short-lived result of an ill-considered act of destruction.

The background: after 1948, therefore some twenty-six years after the conclusion of the Colorado River Compact when the northern bordering states had given their consent to the distribution plan, the Bureau of Reclamation of the Ministry of the Interior department responsible for dam construction presented, in 1953, a list of additional dam projects in the Colorado basin, all in the "upper" basin. Among them was a dam in Glen Canyon and one in Echo Park on the Green River, within today's Dinosaur National Monument. The Echo Park Project was the most attacked and was therefore removed from the list, and the Flaming Gorge Dam in Utah was added in its stead. In the vehement dispute over the Echo Park Dam, Glen Canyon was forgotten, so to speak, and it came about that in 1956 both the Flaming Gorge Dam as well as the Glen Canyon Dam were built.

Criticism of the construction of the Flaming Gorge Dam was never voiced aloud; more strident, however, was the criticism about the Glen Canyon Dam construction. Why? Glen Canyon, 320 kilometres (200 miles) in length, is not only the longest after the Grand Canyon; it was also, according to the experts, the most attractive by far of the numerous Colorado canyons. However, the fact that it could only be reached with great difficulty by land and water-ways earned it the name "the place no one knew", after the decision was made to flood it by building a dam. It is true that only a few persevering hikers, riders and boaters have seen Glen Canyon in its original beauty and their photographs have provided us with a reflection of its splendour, vanished today.

Those who have experienced Glen Canyon have praised it to the limits. John Wesley Powell, the first person to travel the Colorado through Glen Canyon and the Grand Canyon, decidedly a tough fellow to judge by his achievements, used words of the greatest admiration, calling it a tremendous assemblage of magnificent wonders, polished faces, majestic arches, glens, gullies, ramparts and monuments. Powell continued by adding "We have found a gigantic cave scored into the rock. On the upper edge there is a clear, deep pond, bordered by green plants. The cave is over 60 metres (200 feet) high, 150 metres (490 feet) long and 60 metres (200 feet) wide. There is a narrow overhead light in the roof rising through several hundreds of metres of rock. This is where we set up our camp. My

Animals and plants in the Grand Canyon. Above: A flowering specimen of the prickly pear, a cactus species widely distributed in the USA. Middle: Ravens inhabit even the loneliest parts of the canyon. Below: The narrow-leaved popcorn flower (Cryptantha angustifolia) of the blue shrub family.

14

Above: A striped chipmunk, one of the shy, comical rodents whose home is the Grand Canyon. Middle: The brittlebush sunflower species (Encelia farinosa). Below: The mule deer, named for its large ears, is an agile rock climber. The harmless-looking animals defend themselves with their sharp hooves when they feel threatened.

brother sang an evensong, and we listened enthraled as the cave in the rocks filled with sweet tones. It must certainly have been created as a music academy by its storm-born architect; for this reason we have called it the 'Music Temple'." It is questionable whether John Wesley Powell would have consented to have the artificial lake which flooded a place of such magic bear his name.

"Music Temple", "Cathedral in the Desert" and many other places the beauty of which it is difficult to describe. Highly polished, domed faces, decorated with desert lacquer (desert lacquer is the shiny crust of lacquer on sandstone, formed through the leaching of minerals containing iron and manganese, conveyed to the surface by rain-water) and "hanging gardens" (hanging plants fed by seepage), cool, shady places the silence of which is only occasionally broken by wheeling birds. All this has been irretrievably lost, first covered by water then buried by sludge and pebbles. This means that if the dam were to be blown up today ("crack the dam" is the vehement demand of the opponents of the dam, whose goal is to allow the dammed-up water to flow away), the emergent terrain would not have been worth these rescue operations. The rock faces would be bleached a pale grey, for just in these few years the water would have leached away the iron and manganese minerals which give them their colour; the canyon floors, dry again, would be no more than a desert of pebbles and dust. It cannot be predicted whether the newly unleashed Colorado waters would wash clear the canyon floors, and whether the rocks would in time retrieve their original colours. But all this is just nebulous theory, for in practice both the plans as well as the possibility of implementing the removal of the dam are lacking.

Although Glen Canyon is irretrievably lost, visitors to Lake Powell hope that the lake will soon fill to the extent as had been planned. For currently (1992), its level has sunk 25 metres (82 feet), leaving unattractive "bathtub rings" on its banks. The continuous influx of sludge and rocks does indeed reinforce the rising of the water-level, but it will also result in the end of Lake Powell, in some four hundred to one thousand years. But boating will be limited on the lake long before then. New shallows will be formed, and trips in the lake's tributaries, which today give pleasure to so many excursionists, will no longer be possible. Even the entry into Forbidden Canyon, the access to Rainbow Bridge, could then be blocked.

But today, Lake Powell is still a place of perfect enjoyment for millions of holiday-makers, which Glen Canyon could never have been. Desert climate, blue skies, perfect weather for bathing (interrupted in mid-summer by dramatic thunderstorms, the origin of which is favoured by heavy water evaporation), impressive rock façades, deep blue, warm water and excellent water sports possibilities – what more could one want?

The hike along the South Kaibab Trail runs through primeval landscapes into the earth's past.

Flora and Fauna

Considering the barren stony desert landscape seen from the edge of the Grand Canyon, one could doubt the existence of living beings in this area. But the sight deceives: there are more than one thousand plant species here, seventy-five mammal and two hundred-thirty bird species, forty-three amphibian and reptile representatives as well as sixteen fish species!

The fish were the most affected by the construction of Glen Canyon Dam. The Colorado's waters were formerly muddy and of differing seasonal temperatures, but today the waters are clearer and ice-cold the year round, for they are drawn from the bottom of the lake; the temperature is only 10 degrees Celsius (50 degrees Fahrenheit). Trout can live in this; other fish have been driven away.

However, the construction of dams has had no influence on animal and plant worlds in the Grand Canyon. Now as formerly, temperatures of almost 50 degrees Celsius (122 degrees Fahrenheit) have been measured on the canyon floor; on the canyon façades, the temperature drops to below zero degrees Celsius (32 degrees Fahrenheit) in winter, on the South Rim usually only for a few days; on the approximately 400 metre (1,300 foot) higher North Rim, the temperature drops for longer. In winter, metre-deep snow covers the ground sometimes for months on end.

In 1890, C. Hart Merriam, Director of the US Ministry of Agriculture, defined seven climatic and life-supporting areas for the North American continent: tropical, subtropical hot lower Sonoran "life zone", upper Sonoran "life zone", transitional, Canadian, Hudsonian and the arctic-alpine areas. The hiker passes through four of these areas, from the lower Sonoran "life zone" on the canyon floor to the Canadian on the Kaibab Plateau, when he climbs from Phantom Ranch to the North Rim, a trip of approximately twenty-two kilometres (fourteen miles) with a height difference of 1,750 metres (5,740 feet). On such a short trip, the same climatic areas are crossed as those encountered on a 2,800 kilometre- (1,740 mile-) trek from Baja California in Mexico to British Columbia in Canada.

Four climatic areas in the Grand Canyon! It is hardly surprising, then, that the variety of animal and plant species is so great. In the lower Sonoran areas which extend from the canyon floor (760 metres/2,490 feet above sea-level at the Kaibab Suspension Bridge) to the south cliffs up to 1,500 metres (4,920 feet) and to the north cliffs up to 1,200 metres (3,940 feet) above sea-level, living conditions are the most difficult. Plants and animals wishing to survive here must be very frugal and tough and either very inconspicuous and quick, or appear very disconcerting to their enemies. Typical of this climatic area is a bush one to four metres (3.3 to 13 feet) high; named Catclaw, it is equipped

with sharp, hooked thorns. The canyon bat prefers to live here, as well as in the next higher area. This bat is so small that it is often taken for a moth, albeit a very fast one. Other inhabitants of the lower Sonoran area are ringed iguanas which can grow to thirty centimetres (twelve inches). The male of the species ranges from vivid yellow to vivid green, whereas the female displays all shades of grey to vivid orange. The animals owe their name to the light and dark bands around their throats. It seems that these iguanas do not have to hide; their colours probably throw their enemies into confusion. Be prepared as well for scorpions and rattlesnakes.

Above this, in the upper Sonoran zone rising to 2,100 metres (6,888 feet) above sea-level on the south cliffs and to 1,800 metres (5,900 feet) on the north cliffs, the fish-hook cactus is typical, a yellow blooming plant which looks like a small ball equipped with fish hooks. Characteristic of this life sphere are the Utah juniper bushes and the American nut-pine and Umbrella pine, which form the so-called dwarf woods. The first mammals appear in this area: the mountain squirrel and the grey fox.

Larger mammals such as the puma, lynx, wapiti deer, bighorn sheep do not pay much attention to C. Hart Merriam's climatic areas; they cross over them freely. Once, a mule deer was observed descending in one day from the canyon edge to the river, and swimming across it. Then his trail was lost. Did he climb up the other side? This is quite probable, for neither humans nor larger animals can stand being down on the canyon floor for very long.

One distinctive member among the mammals in the great canyon are the burros, wild descendants of the donkeys who formerly conveyed the ore mined in the canyon and who, after mining was stopped, were chased into the wilderness. Their living space reaches from the canyon edge to the river, but they eat the food of the native animals and consequently disturb the balance of nature. Therefore attempts were made time and again to remove the burros, as it is euphemistically expressed, from the Grand Canyon. Today they are usually caught and taken to new homes.

Back to the climatic areas. The upper Sonoran "life zone" is followed by the transitional zone, which extends from the north side of the Grand Canyon to a height of 2,500 metres (8,200 feet). The Ponderosa or yellow pine is typical of this area, as are the Golden-mantled ground squirrel, the Abert and the Kaibab squirrels. The latter are of particular interest to biologists. The Abert squirrel lives only on the South Rim, the Kaibab squirrel only on the North Rim. Both squirrel species feed mainly on the tips of twigs, bark and seeds of the yellow pine, and are therefore dependent on it, as the biologists see it. They have the same build, size and habits, both have dark grey backs with a dark stripe. Then the differences begin: the Abert squirrel has a white belly and a grey tail, the Kaibab has a

While snow and icy winter cold can prevail on the canyon's rim zone, the lower regions of the canyon are characterized by the warmth of their milder climatic zones. The canyon appears unreal and mysterious in the rising fog and with its soft colours in the pale winter light. Views from the South Rim.

The Colorado and its tributaries have created many natural wonders. The Colorado itself created the Grand Canyon, the Glen Canyon, which has since been flooded, as well as the impressive landscapes of the Canyonlands National Park further upstream, jointly with the Green River. Smaller tributaries formed the Escalante Canyon, Paria Canyon, Rainbow Bridge and Havasu Canyon.

Each of these natural wonders is unique in itself, incomparable and yet comparable in a way with other natural monuments of the world. The smallest, most unassuming tributaries of the Colorado, which are drawn only on very detailed maps, have created something for which there is no comparison outside the Colorado Plateau: the Slickrock Canyons, narrow, hidden canyons full of marvels and mystery.

A "slickrock" is a smooth façade of an abyss or canyon. But the term canyon is misleading. The Slickrock Canyons in the

Sandstone formations in Antelope Canyon.

Colorado Plateau have nothing in common with the canyons of the European Alps, for example. The latter are damp, filled with the roaring of water, usually connected by steps and foot-bridges and are therefore easily accessible, and are drawn on most every competent map.

The Slickrock Canyons, on the contrary, are dust dry, deathly silent and quite dangerous in addition: rattlesnakes and more importantly sudden tidal waves

SLICKROCK CANYONS

Mysterious Rock Worlds

Climbing in Antelope Canyon.

after storms occasionally threaten hikers. And they are, or were until recently, "secret". The first people to discover these canyons, some years ago, strenuously attempted to keep their location secret, in an attempt to conserve the natural solitude and beauty of the setting.

But what are these Slickrock Canyons, which are still not mentioned in many of today's guide books? It is difficult, even impossible, to describe them. How can one describe sandstone caves lit with diffuse, indirect light – as cathedrals in stone? The elegant soft ridges of the wall – as flowing rock? Is there anything comparable to the twists of a labyrinth? In addition to this, the human eye can only imperfectly perceive these forms, for the natural lighting in the Slickrock Canyons is usually quite low.

The real beauty of the shapes and colours, from light yellow, orange, red, blue to black, is visible only in time exposure photographs taken with a tripod. Consequently, the Slickrock Canyons are above all an eldorado for committed and well-equipped photographers, especially when the partially concealed secret is finally fully revealed, that is, the exact location of the most beautiful among them, the Antelope Canyon.

A first reference to its existence is provided by Antelope Creek southeast of Page, Arizona. This stream, which only exists after heavy rainfall, but which is then very dangerous, flows to the north into Lake Powell near Antelope Island. Incidentally, the creek is drawn only on rather detailed maps of the region.

The starting point for visits to Antelope Canyon is the second bridge on Highway 89 from Page to Kaibito, just before the power station with its gigantic shiny chimneys visible over a wide area. An approximately six kilometre- (four mile-) long track leads from here, through deep sand in some stretches, towards the south to a divided petrified dune twelve metres (forty feet) high.

One can saunter through this upper section of Antelope Canyon, also called Corkscrew Canyon or The Crack, and easily reach the sixty metres (two hundred feet) leading to the exit on the other side of the dunes. The middle section is just as

Dangerous, but shy: the rattlesnake.

easy to reach; it is situated directly below the above-mentioned bridge. When one has come as far as this, it is no longer a problem to reach the lower section. Simply follow the bed of the Antelope Creek to the north, until a small opening in the sandstone appears, some fifty metres (one hundred-sixty-four feet) further on. Although it seems unbelievable at first glance, this trail leads into a sinuous wonderworld, conveying totally different impressions than those of the first two sections of the canyon.

Admittedly, one is obliged here to lower oneself on a rope over steep terraces five to ten metres (sixteen to thirty-three feet) high and to wade through hip-deep ponds. Usually, however, there are some Navajo Indians around this area who will help out with ladders and ropes for a modest tip. What may initially seem like quite a lot of inconvenience becomes, in the end, an adventure. And the Slickrock Canyons are definitely worth it!

Helmut Friedrich

Antelope Canyon. The impassable and difficult to find Slickrock Canyons, absolute natural wonders hidden in the rock, reward visitors with almost unreal colours and rock formations in diffuse light, a bizarre underground labyrinth, formed over thousands of years by water-borne sediment.

black belly and a white tail. It almost seems as if an animal species already existing before the creation of the Grand Canyon had developed into different sub-species. Then the presence of the great canyon led to a division into two groups, no longer permitting exchanges between the two particularly because of climatological barriers. But why in the way just described? No answer to this puzzle has as yet been forthcoming.

One suggested explanation is that the Kaibab squirrel's white tail results from adaptation to the snow which lies on the North Rim from November to May; this explanation, however, does not fit the facts. The dark grey body of the animal does not offer any camouflage in the snow, and the animal does not place its tail over its back when it gets wind of danger. Also, the tail remains white the whole year round; therefore, it is more of a signal in snow-free periods, but by no stretch of the imagination does it have a camouflage function.

On the North Rim of the canyon, the transitional area joins the Canadian area, which begins at approximately 2,500 metres (8,200 feet) above sea-level. The Colorado fir and the Douglas fir grow here, trees which prefer coolness and moisture. The Douglas fir can also be found scattered on the South Rim (although it is beneath the Canadian area) where there are shady, cool places, where the local climate resembles the Canadian area. A good example of how the climatic areas in the Grand Canyon cannot be delineated with a straight-edge.

In autumn in the North Rim area, the American aspen is particularly striking, with its many gold- and brown-toned leaves glowing and trembling in the breeze. It is a truly unforgettable sight. An animal often encountered here is the playful mule deer: in the late afternoon, whole herds emerge from the woods to graze in the meadows and leap across the roads in a carefree manner, so that motorists must be very alert.

Saurians in the Grand Canyon?

The above described evolution of the squirrels on both sides of the canyon caused the question to be raised as to whether such independent developments could be found on the buttes rising isolated from the Grand Canyon. In 1937 an expedition led by the curator of the American Museum of Natural History, Harold Anthony, was planned. The goal was the Shiva Temple, a high, wooded butte separated from the North Rim some 20,000 years ago by erosion. Hardly had their intentions been made known when the newspapers began speculating whether dinosaurs could be living "up there". However, right from the start, Anthony had not hoped for anything more than the discovery of minor mutations of known species, perhaps an additional squirrel species.

Because it was at first assumed that the butte could not be climbed, a helicopter landing was discussed, but this idea was soon dropped because of expected dangerous air currents; for the same reason the idea of parachuting was also discounted. It was not until it was finally decided to climb the mountain that it became evident that the summit was relatively easy to ascend. The expedition needed only a morning to climb the last 400 metres (1,300 feet) from an easily accessible saddle at the foot of the mountain. This obviously led to the suspicion that nothing new would be found here, for the conditions for species isolation were not fulfilled.

This suspicion was confirmed. After several days of thorough searching for evidence on the plateau, the research group found a deer's antler shed in the same year as the expedition, as well as fresh puma and coyote tracks. Small live animals such as mountain rats and chipmunks which they trapped did not differ from their "cousins" on the North Rim.

All the buttes in the canyon have not yet been climbed; there is still hope, although in very small measure, of finding isolated life forms. But they will certainly not be dinosaurs or dragons.

A Ramble Through the Past

The Grand Canyon can be discovered in various ways: on foot, on mule-back, in a boat or from the air. However, a peaceful descent into the canyon is indisputably the best way to discover its climatic areas and inhabitants. This path also leads through earth's history, a journey through two billion – meaning 2,000 million – years.

This past is already revealed on the canyon's edge: when taking his first steps, the hiker walks on 225 million-year-old rocks – deposits of an ocean which formerly covered this area. An ocean at the height of 2,000 metres (6,560 feet)? Former ocean beds at this height are geological proof of the Colorado Plateau's rising, which continued over millions of years and which ended only ten million years ago. The original lowland plain was raised some 3,000 metres (9,840 feet), of which 1,500 metres (5,000 feet) have been carried off in the last ten million years. This is how 225 million-year-old sediment came to be at mountain level.

Just how big a step into the earth's past is taken by the hiker can be made clear by a simple consideration: the trip from the South Rim to the Kaibab Suspension Bridge is approximately twelve kilometres (seven-and-a-half miles), a place where the rocks are over two billion years old. Each step, therefore, spans some one hundred-thousand years of the earth's history!

Up to a height of approximately 300 metres (1,000 feet) above the river one crosses over a series of ten sediment

The South Kaibab Trail. In the past, some forty paths ran down into the canyon. They were laid by Indians, gold-miners or mine-owners; however, the majority of them have been abandoned and are impassable today. Only Bright Angel Trail and Kaibab Trail are maintained by the National Parks administration.

The scale and splendour of the canyon can best be discovered during a tranquil journey into the depths – on the back of a mule...

layers on the hiking path, the oldest of which originated in the Cambrian Period and are therefore some 550 million years old. These are not only ocean deposits: the layers of dune and river deposits encountered are proof of varied and dynamic geological development processes. On this spot, however, one step straddles 650 million years, for abruptly following the 550 million-year-old sandstone are the 1,200 year-old granite and gneiss. And finally, on the banks of the Colorado River, the two billion year-old Vishnu slate, the remains of an ancient mountain, becomes visible.

The long journey into the abyss offers the opportunity to understand better the dimensions of this colossal chasm. The question inevitably is raised: was it really the Colorado, which from above appears so inconspicuous and at Lee's Ferry appears so sluggish, which created this canyon, and within "only" four to ten million years? (So great are the differences in estimates among geologists). It would be easier to imagine if one could experience the former power of the Colorado when in full spate.

But there is no other explanation for it: the Grand Canyon is the work of the Colorado and its tributaries. Of course, the river and its little helpers were not alone in this. The canyon had to be more "neatly worked over". Its bizarre jagged form indicates on the one hand that addi-

tional forces were at work and on the other hand that particular conditions were required for its creation.

By forces we mean the weathering of exposed rocks, the explosive power of frozen water and the force of gravity which allowed the banks formed by the river to slide away. By conditions we mean the existing geological conditions in the canyon such as fissures, warping and the differing degrees of hardness of the comparatively soft, crumbly rock layers, which afforded a good starting point for attacks by the aggressive river.

In other words: the canyon was not formed by the river's persistent milling and grinding, but rather through the numerous rock falls and landslides which the Colorado and its tributaries induced and through the detritus which they then cleared away. Just what the Colorado can perform when carrying matter away has already been described. The Colorado became active with milling, grinding and polishing only after reaching hard granite and slate. It will continue working on this increasingly, if the dams which slow its course are no longer obstacles and as long as there are no more gradients from the outlet of the Grand Canyon to the Gulf of California. When will that be? We will not experience this in our lifetime nor that of our children and grandchildren, but in geological times it will be as tomorrow.

...or during a hike, such as here on the South Kaibab Trail. On the rock façade, the various layers can be differentiated: the white Toroweap limestone, the darker Coconino sandstone, the reddish Hermit slate and Supai sandstone, and the grey Muav limestone.

A SPECTACLE TOO STRANGE TO BE REAL
Reports of the Grand Canyon

"I have never witnessed anything like this. It scares me to even try to look down into it. My God, I am afraid the whole country will fall into this great hole in the ground." This inscription, written in a visitors' book in the 1890's, is not much different from the opinions one hears today at the Grand Canyon: waves of superlatives and allusions to the canyon as proof of God's presence. Some visitors are simply terrified. Surprisingly, the most common response seems to be little reaction at all. One American official, after a minute of silent reflection, turned to his guide and said, "Let's have a cup of coffee." Whatever it is that one first feels, the Grand Canyon is not easy to comprehend, as the following texts will show.

The Coronado Expedition

As Don Pedro de Tovar had no other commission, he returned from Tusayán and gave his report to the general. The latter at once dispatched Don García López de Cárdenas there with about twelve men to explore this river. When he reached Tusayán he was well received and lodged by the natives. They provided him with guides to proceed on his journey. They set out from there laden with provisions, because they had to travel over some uninhabited land before coming to settlements, which the Indians said were more than twenty days away.

Accordingly when they had marched for twenty days they came to the gorges of the river, from the edge of which it looked as if the opposite side must have been more than three or four leagues away by air. This region was high and covered with low and twisted pine trees; it was extremely cold, being open to the north, so that, although this was the warm season, no one could live in this canyon because of the cold.

The men spent three days looking for a way down to the river; from the top it looked as if the water were a fathom across. But, according to the information supplied by the Indians, it must have been half a league wide. The descent was almost impossible, but, after these three days, at a place which seemed less difficult, Captain Melgosa, a certain Juan Galeras, and another companion, being the most agile, began to go down. They continued descending within view of those on top until they lost sight of them, as they could not be seen from the top.

They returned about four o'clock in the afternoon, as they could not reach the bottom because of the many obstacles they met, for what from the top seemed easy, was not so; on the contrary, it was rough and difficult. They said that they had gone down one-third of the distance and that, from the point they had reached, the river seemed very large, and that, from what they saw, the width given by the Indians was correct. From the top they could make out, apart from the canyon, some small boulders which seemed to be as high as a man. Those who went down and who reached them swore that they were taller than the great tower of Seville.

The party did not continue farther up the canyon of the river because of the lack of water. Up to that time they had gone one or two leagues inland in search of water every afternoon. When they had traveled four additional days the guides said that it was impossible to go on because no water would be found for three or four days, that when they themselves traveled through that land they took along women who brought water in gourds, that in those trips they buried the gourds of water for the return trip, and that they traveled in one day a distance that took us two days.

This was the Tízon river, much closer to its source than where Melchior Díaz and his men had crossed it. These Indians were of the same type, as it appeared later. From there Cárdenas and his men turned back, as that trip brought no other results.

On the way they saw a waterfall which came down a rock. They learned from the guides that some clusters which hung like fine crystals were salt. They went thither and gathered quantities of it which they brought and distributed when they returned to Cíbola.

FRANCISCO VÁSQUEZ DE CORONADO's men located the Grand Canyon in 1540. Though they attempted to cross it, after several days without water, they were forced to turn back. The Grand Canyon then remained unexplored for two centuries, until the arrival of Christian missionaries.

Marble Canyon

This part of Marble Cañon, from Point Retreat for thirty-five miles down to the Little Colorado, is by far the most beautiful and interesting cañon we have yet passed through. At Point Retreat the marble walls stand perpendicularly 300 feet from the water's edge, while the sandstone above benches back in slopes and cliffs to 2,500 feet high. Just below this the cañon is narrowest, being but a little over 300 feet from wall to wall. As we go on, the marble rapidly rises till it stands in perpendicular cliffs 700 to 800 feet high, colored with all the tints of the rainbow, but mostly red. In many places toward the top it is honeycombed with caves, arches, and grottoes, with here and there a natural bridge left from one crag to another over some sidewash, making a grotesque and wonderful picture as our little boats glide along this quiet portion of the river, so many hundred feet below.

At the foot of these cliffs, in many places, are fountains of pure sparkling water gushing from the rock – in one place, Vasey's Paradise, several hundred feet up the wall – and dropping among shrubbery, ferns, and flowers, some of which even at this time of year are found in bloom.

Ten miles below Point Retreat, as we went into camp one evening, we discovered the body of Peter M. Hansbrough, one of the boatmen drowned on our trip last summer. His remains were easily recognized from the clothing that was still on them. The next morning we buried them under an overhanging cliff. The burial service was brief and simple. We stood around the grave while one short prayer was offered, and we left him with a shaft of pure marble for his headstone, seven hundred feet high, with his name cut upon the base; and in honor of his memory we named a magnificent point opposite – Point Hansbrough.

In the late nineteenth century, a Denver capitalist named Frank Brown organized the Denver Railway Company and hired ROBERT BREWSTER STANTON as the chief engineer. Together, they started down the Colorado River to survey a "water level" railroad through the river's canyons from the Rocky Mountains to California. The survey party was ill-prepared for the journey, and after three drownings in one week, including President Brown's, the task was abandoned.

Flora …

Although we reached the plateau in mid-July, the spring was but just coming to an end. Silver-voiced Rocky Mountain hermit-thrushes chanted divinely from the deep woods. There were multitudes of flowers, of which, alas! I know only a very few, and these by their vernacular names; for as yet there is no such handbook for the flowers of the

Above and below: On the South Kaibab Trail. This path usually offers clear visibility and spectacular vistas. Its construction took four years, from 1924 to 1928. This path leads hikers down to the Colorado River and up again to the North Rim (as the North Kaibab Trail).

southern Rocky Mountains. ... The sego lilies, looking like very handsome Eastern trilliums, were as plentiful as they were beautiful; and there were the striking Indian paint-brushes, fragrant purple locust blooms, the blossoms of that strange bush the plumed acacia, delicately beautiful, white columbines, bluebells, great sheets of blue lupin, and the tall, crowded spikes of the brilliant red bell – and innumerable others. The rainfall is light and the ground porous; springs are few, and brooks wanting; but the trees are handsome. In a few places the forest is dense; in most places it is sufficiently open to allow a mountain-horse to twist in and out among the tree trunks at a smart canter. The tall yellow pines are everywhere; the erect spires of the mountain-spruce and of the blue-tipped Western balsam shoot up around their taller cousins, and the quaking asps, the aspens with their ever-quivering leaves and glimmering white boles, are scattered among and beneath the conifers, or stand in groves by themselves.

Blue grouse were plentiful – having increased greatly, partly because of the war waged by Uncle Jim against their foes the great horned owls; and among the numerous birds were long-crested, dark-blue jays, pinyon-jays, doves, band-tailed pigeons, golden-winged flickers, chickadees, juncos, mountain-bluebirds, thistle-finches, and Louisiana tanagers. A very handsome cock tanager, the orange yellow of its plumage dashed with red on the head and throat, flew familiarly round Uncle Jim's cabin, and spent most of its time foraging in the grass. Once three birds flew by which I am convinced were the strange and interesting evening grosbeaks. Chipmunks and white-footed mice lived in the cabin, the former very bold and friendly; in fact, the chipmunks, of several species, were everywhere; and there were gophers or rock-squirrels, and small tree-squirrels, like the Eastern chickarees, and big tree-squirrels – the handsomest squirrels I have ever seen – with black bodies and bushy white tails. These last lived in the pines, were diurnal in their habits, and often foraged among the fallen cones on the ground; they were strikingly conspicuous.

THEODORE ROOSEVELT is perhaps the most famous of the Grand Canyon's cougar hunters. As president, he established the North Kaibab Game Preserve and proclaimed the Grand Canyon a national monument. Roosevelt wrote the above text during the summer of 1913.

... and Fauna

The most striking and best known example of two closely related animals which, for many thousands of years, have been kept separate by the Canyon is that of the Kaibab and the Abert squirrels which happen to be the handsomest representatives of their family in the United States and likely to win admiring attention from any traveler who sees either the one or the other, even though he knows nothing of their story.

Both are large, noticeably larger than the eastern gray squirrel. Both also have rich, reddish-brown backs, handsome ear tufts or tassels which appear only in winter and huge fluffy tails providing a panache extravagant even for a squirrel. But they are also strikingly different. The Abert has a white belly and a grayish tail; the Kaibab a black belly and an astonishing pure white plume behind. The first is the commoner, occurring in isolated but favorable mountain areas south of the Canyon and scattered over both the Southwestern United States and northern Mexico. The Kaibab is restricted to an island plateau some twenty by forty miles in extent, which is the northern half of the dome through which the Canyon is cut and which is isolated, not only by the Canyon to the south, but by deserts to the east, and west and the north. In that restricted area he is by no means uncommon. Sometimes he is seen around the north rim camp grounds, though in my experience the surest place to see him for either aesthetic or scientific reasons, is in the great forest of pines at Jacob Lake, through which all visitors headed for the north rim must pass.

The habits of the Abert and the Kaibab are essentially identical, and both are restricted vertically as well as horizontally. All live in the region of high pines at six to eight thousand feet, making only rare forays a short distance down to the live-oak region or a short distance up to the firs. Sometimes they inhabit tree holes but mostly they build bushel-sized homes of leaves lined with grass or bark and put high in the trees where, in bad weather, the inhabitants may stay for a week or ten days at a time. They have the engaging habit of transporting their young under their bellies, tail between their forelegs and with the baby holding on for dear life. They store little food, and though they sometimes rummage around the ground for seeds and tubers, they are wholly dependent for their main food supply on the living inner bark of the pine tree – principally the ponderosa. In winter they climb out to the ends of small branches, cut them off, and then, on the ground, gnaw through to the nourishing layer where life is still going on.

A retired professor of dramatic literature, JOSEPH WOOD KRUTCH devoted his later years to the protection of the desert environment. His literature and natural philosophy belong to the tradition established by Henry Thoreau.

Havasu Creek

Below our camp a quarter of a mile, past a field half overgrown with apparently wild squash vines and the dark green datura, the Western Jimson weed, with its great white

The Grand Can-
yon presents a
completely differ-
ent face in winter:
snow-covered trees
and rocks on the
South Rim. The
abyss is veiled in a
mysterious mist,
appearing distant
and inaccessible.

trumpet-flowers, Havasu Creek takes a second fall. Apart from its name, Bridal Veil, it is more than satisfactory, for it spreads wide along the ledge and falls in four or five streamers down a hundred-foot cliff clothed in exotic hanging plants and curtains of travertine. The cliff is green and gray and orange, the pool below pure cobalt, and below the pool the creek gathers itself in terraces bordered with green cress.

A little below the fall a teetery suspension footbridge hangs over a deep green pool, dammed by a terrace so smooth that the water pours over it in a shining sheet like milky blue glass. And down another half mile, after a suc-

cession of pools each of which leaves us more incredulous, the stream leaps in an arching curve over Mooney Falls, the highest of the three. At its foot are the same tall cottonwoods with dusty red bark, the same emerald basin, the same terraced pools flowing away, and below the pools is another suspension footbridge on which we sit to eat lunch and converse with a friendly tree toad.

It is a long way to the mouth of the canyon, where Havasu Creek falls into the Colorado in the lower end of Grand Canyon. We stop at the abandoned lead and copper mine below Mooney Falls, where we ponder the strength of the compulsion that would drive men to bring heavy machinery piecemeal down into this pocket on the backs of horses, set it up under incredible difficulties, construct an elaborate water system and a cluster of houses and sheds, bore into the solid cliffs for ore, and then tote the ore back out miles to some road where trucks could get it. The very thought gives us packhorse feet, and we make our way back to camp, yielding to temptation at every pool on the creek until we have a feeling that our skins are beginning to harden with a thin sheath of lime. After a day, we are beginning to realize how truly paradisiac the home of the Havasupai is.

There are in the West canyons as colorful and as beautiful as Havasu, with walls as steep and as high, with floors as verdantly fertile. There are canyons more spectacularly narrow and more spectacularly carved. But I know of none, except possibly Oak Creek Canyon south of Flagstaff, which has such bewitching water. In this country the mere presence of water, even water impregnated with red mud, is much. But water in such lavish shining streams, water so extravagantly colorful, water which forms such terraces and pools, water which all along its course nourishes plants that give off that mysterious wonderful smell like witch hazel, water which obliges by forming three falls, each more beautiful than the last, is more than one has a right to expect.

In the 1940's, WALLACE STEGNER took a horseback trip down to Havasu, a side-canyon Shangri-La inhabited by several hundred Indians. Stegner's book "Beyond the Hundreth Meridian" is a definitive assessment of John Wesley Powell and his scientific accomplishments in the west.

The Heritage of the Desert

When he awakened, the fire was low, and he was numb with cold. He took care to put on logs enough to last until morning; then, he lay down once more, but did not sleep. The dawn came with a gray morning shade in the forest; it was a cloud, and it rolled over him soft, tangible, moist, and cool, and passed away under the pines. With its vanishing, the dawn lightened.

"Mescal, if we're on the spur of Coconina, it's only ten miles or so to Silver Cup," said Hare, as he saddled Silvermane. "Mount, now, and we'll go up out of the hollow and get our bearings."

While ascending the last step to the rim, Hare revolved in his mind the probabilities of marking a straight course to Silver Cup.

"Oh, Jack!" exclaimed Mescal suddenly. "Vermillion Cliffs and home!"

"I've traveled in a circle!" replied Hare.

Mescal was enraptured at the scene, as her gaze signified. Vermillion Cliffs shone red as a rose. The split in the wall, marking the oasis, defined its outlines sharply against

Left page: Snow-covered pines on the canyon rim.

Above and below: Winter on the South Rim of the canyon. Hoar frost, snow and a sky of clouds create soft, flowing colours and forms which evoke India ink paintings of the Far East.

On the Grand Canyon's North Rim: mighty rock terraces stand out with their thin layers of snow.

the sky. Miles of the Colorado River lay in sight. Hare knew he stood on the highest point of Coconina overhanging the cañon and the Painted Desert, thousands of feet below. He sighted the wondrous abyss sleeping in blue mist at his feet while he gazed across to the desert awakening in the first red rays of the rising sun.

Sand – lava – plain – mesa – were mere colored dots and streaks in space, softening aspects of a marginless waste, purple details that led the eye to where a dim horizon merged in the heavens. The same alluring desert, yet how different! He had felt its dry teeth in his life; he had crossed it; he knew its deceiving distances; still was it a mystery.

He followed the Little Colorado winding down through the Painted Desert to join the great river, and his survey brough the chasm directly under his eye. He echoed Mescal's exclamation, and, reaching for her hand, held it while he tried to comprehend the awe-inspiring spectacle. He stood on the edge of a ruined world of stone. Where was the sea that had not been filled by the silt washed from this gap? The huge domes, the escarpments, the pinnacles and turrets were draped in gray. Deep, dark blue marked the clefts between the mesas, and the tips of the crags caught the rose of the sun. There were no sudden changes, no sudden breaks – all the millions of slopes and terraces merged together, enfolded in soft haze, soft mist, soft cloud, in one soft effect of entrancing beauty.

ZANE GREY's two best novels are based in the American Southwest. This excerpt is taken from a 1910 story in which the heroine, Mescal, spends a year hidden in a remote canyon oasis to escape danger at the hands of vicious outlaws. As the plot later turns in favour of the hero, he rides to Thunder River to rescue her. The story's fictional river crossing is as memorable as any scene from the journals of real-life river runners.

A Day in the Canyon

August 14. At daybreak we walk down the bank of the river, on a little sandy beach, to take a view of a new feature in the cañon. Heretofore, hard rocks have given us bad river; soft rocks, smooth water; and a series of rocks harder than any we have experienced sets in. The river enters the granite!

We can see but a little way into the granite gorge, but it looks threatening. After breakfast we enter on the waves. At the very introduction, it inspires awe.

The cañon is narrower than we have ever before seen it; the water is swifter; there are but few broken rocks in the channel; but the walls are set, on either side, with pinnacles and crags; and sharp, angular buttresses bristling with wind and wave polished spires, extend far out into the river. Ledges of rocks jut into the stream, their tops sometimes just below the surface, sometimes rising few or

Colourful vegetation in the canyon's rocky landscape. Above: The agave, also called the maguey or century plant. Middle: cacti which captivate by the beauty of their flowers, such as the claret cup. Bottom: A cactus called Echinocereus triglochidiatus engelmannii and wild flowers.

Little Colorado River Canyon. John Wesley Powell, leader of the maiden journey down the river in 1875, described the Little Colorado as a very small river, exceedingly muddy and salty. The canyon from which it flows into the Colorado is almost as splendid as that of the main river.

35

Vivid colours and bizarre shadows on the bleak surface of the rocks. A view from Hopi Point onto the deep Colorado, some 1,750 metres (5,740 feet) below…

many feet above; and island ledges, and island pinnacles, and island towers break the swift course of the stream into chutes, and eddies, and whirlpools.

We soon reach a place where a creek comes in from the left, and just below, the channel is choked with boulders which have washed down this lateral cañon and formed a dam, over which there is a fall of thirty or forty feet; but on the boulders we can get foothold, and we make a portage.

Three more such dams are found. Over one we make a portage; at the other two we find chutes, through which we can run.

As we proceed, the granite rises higher, until nearly a thousand feet of the lower part of the walls are composed of this rock.

About eleven o'clock we hear a great roar ahead, and approach it very cautiously. The sound grows louder and louder as we run, and at last we find ourselves above a long, broken fall, with ledges and pinnacles of rock obstructing the river. There is a descent of, perhaps, seventy-five of eighty feet in a third of a mile, and the rushing waters break into great waves on the rocks, and lash themselves into a mad, white foam. We can land just above, but there is no foothold on either side by which we can make a portage. It is nearly a thousand feet to the top of the granite, so it will be impossible to carry our boats around,

though we can climb to the summit up a side gulch, and, passing along a mile or two, can descend to the river. This we find on examination; but such a portage would be impracticable for us, and we must run the rapid, or abandon the river. There is no hesitation. We step into our boats, push off and away we go, first on smooth but swift water, then we strike a glassy wave, and ride to its top, down again into the trough, up again on a higher wave, and down and up on waves higher and still higher, until we strike one just as it curls back, and a breaker rolls over our little boat. Still, on we speed, shooting past projecting rocks, till the little boat is caught in a whirlpool, and spun around several times. At last we pull out again into the stream, and now the other boats have passed us. The open compartment of the "Emma Dean" is filled with water, and every breaker rolls over us. Hurled back from a rock, now on this side, now on that, we are carried into an eddy, in which we struggle for a few minutes, and are then out again, the breakers still rolling over us. Our boat is unmanageable, but she cannot sink, and we drift down another hundred yards, through breakers; how, we scarcely know. We find the other boats have turned into an eddy at the foot of the fall, and are waiting to catch us as we come, for the men have seen that our boat is swamped. They push out as we come near, and pull

…the different rock layers show ever new, virtually unreal colours through the constantly changing play of light during the day. A view from Powell Memorial on the South Rim.

us in against the wall. We bail our boat, and on we go again.

The walls, now, are more than a mile in height – a vertical distance difficult to appreciate. Stand on the south steps of the Treasury building, in Washington, and look down Pennsylvania Avenue to the Capitol Park, and measure this distance overhead, and imagine cliffs to extend to that altitude, and you will understand what I mean; or, stand at Canal street, in New York, and look up Broadway to Grace Church, and you have about the distance; or, stand at Lake street bridge, in Chicago, and look down to the Central Depot, and you have it again.

A thousand feet of this is up through granite crags, then steep slopes and perpendicular cliffs rise, one above another, to the summit. The gorge is black and narrow below, red and gray and flaring above, with crags and angular projections on the walls, which, cut in many places by side cañons, seem to be a vast wilderness of rocks. Down in these grand, gloomy depths we glide, ever listening, for the mad waters keep up their roar; ever watching, ever peering ahead, for the narrow cañon is winding, and the river is closed in so that we can see but a few hundred yards, and what there may be below we know not; but we listen for falls, and watch for rocks, or stop now and then, in the bay of a recess, to admire the gigantic scen-

ery. And ever, as we go, there is some new pinnacle or tower, some crag or peak, some distant view of the upper plateau, some strange-shaped rock, or some deep, narrow side cañon. Then we come to another broken fall, which appears more difficult than the one we ran this morning.

A small creek comes in on the right, and the first fall of the water is over the boulders, which have been carried down by this lateral stream. We land at its mouth, and stop for an hour or two to examine the fall. It seems possible to let down with lines, at least a part of the way, from point to point, along the right-hand wall. So we make a portage over the first rocks, and find footing on some boulders below. Then we let down one of the boats to the end of her line, when she reaches a corner of the projecting rock, to which one of the men clings, and steadies her, while I examine an eddy below. I think we can pass the other boats down by us, and catch them in the eddy. This is soon done and the men in the boats in the eddy pull us to their side.

On the shore of this little eddy there is about two feet of gravel beach above the water. Standing on this beach, some of the men take the line of the little boat and let it drift down against another projecting angle. Here is a little shelf on which a man from my boat climbs, and a shorter line is passed to him, and he fastens the boat to the side of

37

continued on page 42

LIFE IN AN OASIS

The Havasu Canyon

Why is it that one can reach the most beautiful places on our earth only at a great cost of time and effort? Toroweap lookout, the floor of the Grand Canyon as well as Havasu Canyon, for example. Why do so many travellers take the trouble to follow the arduous path down into the canyon itself? What makes remote areas such as Cataract Canyon so attractive to visitors?

Some of them are probably interested in the Havasupai Indians living there, the "people of the blue-green water". This is what they are called by the "haigu", the Whites. They call themselves simply Supai. This is also the name of the canyon village in which approximately one hundred of the roughly four hundred members of the Indian tribe live in a relatively isolated way, practising modest agriculture according to traditional methods. The Havasupai have also maintained some old traditions such as the sweat hut, the Indian sauna. It is not only for cleaning the body, but also has a spiritual character. Hunting ceremonies and burial rites have also been retained.

However, most visitors come for the natural beauty of the Havasu Canyon: it conceals a river oasis, unexpected in this limestone desert. After a long journey

Havasupai Indians.

over dry rocky terrain, hikers are welcomed by the sound of rushing water. And finally, after the last bend in the path, there suddenly appears a refreshing green of poplars, fruit trees, bushes and meadows which are irrigated by the Havasu Creek, a crystal clear stream with abundant water which owes its vivid blue colour to the minerals it leaches from the surrounding rocks. As well, since tourism and the developement of the area have been limited by natural factors, the stream has not suffered from the effects of modern-day pollution.

Below the village of Supai are the four famous waterfalls of the Havasu Creek, the Navajo, Havasu, Mooney, and Beaver Falls. The Mooney Falls, the highest amongst them at sixty metres (two hundred feet), were originally called "mother of the waters" by the Indians. The name they bear today is in honour of the ore-miner James Mooney, who wanted in 1880 to lower himself on a rope from the edge of the waterfall to explore the area, but died in the attempt.

The thirty metre- (one hundred foot-) high Havasu Falls are formed of four water branches. The particular delight of their visitors are the basins at their foot, captured by walls of travertine (calcareous tufa); the basins range in size from that of a bathtub to that of a swimming pool. In the cool waters here one can swim as if in a whirlpool.

Interestingly enough, the spray from the falls, blown for centuries against the rocks, has hardened into "stone shower curtains". Whirlpools in the desert, surrounded by lush greenery. These are some of the numerous and unusual aspects of the Colorado's Grand Canyon.

Helmut Friedrich

At the foot of Havasu Falls, large basins of travertine entice tired hikers to a refreshing swim.

The 30 metre- (98 foot-) high Havasu Falls, the most impressive of the four waterfalls in Havasu Canyon. The water contains calcium carbonate which hardens into travertine (calcareous tufa).

Houseboats on Lake Powell: the gigantic Colorado River reservoir is a popular vacation resort.

the cliff. Then the second one is let down, bringing the line of the third. When the second boat is tied up, the two men standing on the beach above spring into the last boat, which is pulled up alongside of ours. Then we let down the boats, for twenty-five or thirty yards, by walking along the shelf, landing them again in the mouth of a side cañon. Just below this there is another pile of boulders, over which we make another portage. From the foot of these rocks we can climb to another shelf, forty or fifty feet above the water.

On this bench we camp for the night. We find a few sticks, which have lodged in the rocks. It is raining hard, and we have no shelter, but kindle a fire and have our supper. We sit on the rocks all night, wrapped in our ponchos, getting what sleep we can.

JOHN WESLEY POWELL first travelled down the Colorado River in 1869; he subsequently made two summer field trips in the Grand Canyon in 1867 and 1868. His personal account of the tours was written in 1874 for serial publication in "Scribner's Monthly". This diary entry was written in 1869.

A Descent to the River

The best thing to do was to descend to the bottom of the Canyon; one must not only look at it but make contact with it as well, and live in it for a whole day at least. At the hotel we hired blue slacks, coats and gloves. The mules were standing in a small enclosure, guarded by two cowboys, whose clothes were a bit too showy; they select mounts suitable to our height and helped us climp into the saddle. There were about a dozen of us on this expedition. One of the cowboys took the head, the other followed in rear. We were photographed in a line at the top of the path: the photographs would await us on our return. Below, a caravan of four mules laden with hay went down the path cut in the rock. Then we began to descend. A notice warned us on departure that it was forbidden to bring dogs. The mules walked with even paces; at each turning they lurched blindly towards the precipice and swung back at the last moment, quietly regaining the middle of the path: at the end of an hour one was used to it. From time to time a placard informed us of the geological age we had reached; they pointed out, too, fossilised shells and ferns. from top to bottom of the path telephone kiosks had been planted and one could amuse oneself by telephoning New York.

We went down slowly, far slower than walking pace. Little by little the scene changed, became more real. We had left the cliff and were crossing a plateau covered with thorny tufts, which from above had been merely a coloured surface; now it had thickness and smell, and each separate tuft existed, while the shades of blue would vary.

After three hours we stopped at the edge of the flat rocks which fall to the river below: from above it appeared as a thin, brilliant thread, but from here it was a torrent with broad waters, swift-flowing, tempting and dangerous; if I should bathe in them they would change colour again. But we never got as far. We halted higher up near some water. The mules ate hay while we had our sandwiches and I dozed for a while in the sun. No time to sleep, however; instead of this expedition one would have liked to walk alone for a long time along these paths, sleep at the water's edge, and follow the river for nights on end on foot or by canoe: to live in the intimacy of the Grand Canyon. This intimacy must be difficult to achieve, for the beauty of the place is at first too beautiful; no doubt its more precious secrets are not easily learnt. But I envy those to whom they have been revealed.

The French feminist, philosopher and novelist SIMONE DE BEAUVOIR toured the United States in 1947, delivering lectures on the moral problems of the post-war writer. Her critical impressions of the country were published as America Day by Day.

A Symphony of Color

Why, many a man has hardly noticed shapes in it at all. They are merely blobs of color. Color so rich and rampant that it floods the whole chasm; so powerful that it dissolves like acid all the shapes within it. Here, if you will, is a drama whose characters are colors: the royal purples, the angry reds, the mellow russets and monkish browns, soothing blues, shrieking yellows, tragic blacks and mystic whites, cool greens, pale lavenders and anemic grays.

A lifetime is too short to watch their infinite variations in key and tone. They change with every season, every hour, and with every change in light and weather.

In the blinding glare of a summer's noon its tints are so muted that the cañon seems a delicate pastel. But watch it at sunset. The yellows slowly deepen to orange; the salmon pinks to reds; the greens and blue-grays to damson blue; the lilacs to purple. Sunrise reverses the process. The whole chasm lifts bodily, inch by inch, toward light. The paint pot tips and spills over. The colors run and seep down the walls, collecting in pools below.

If it is a picture, winter frames it best. Preferably after a heavy snowfall when the plateaus are solid white, and better yet when every twig and needle is still sheathed in ice. Deeply inset in such a frame the cañon has all the warmth and color of a child's stereopticon slice held up to the table lamp. Into it snow never descends. A summer rainstorm is more potent. Then mists and clouds are formed below. Like tiny puffs from father's pipe they spurt out of the warm cañons and swelling like balloons gradually float to surface.

The Colorado River holds a firm place in the mythology of the Indian tribes living in the Grand Canyon area. The Navajos, the Hualapai and the Havasupai believe it is the remains of a great floodwater which once covered the entire earth. A Ute myth, on the contrary, recounts that the river was put into the abyss by a god, to conceal the path to heaven.

An evening idyll: the hazy silhouette of the mountains and the Grate on the South Rim in the gentle mist.

But the cold, clear, cloudless days of October – that is its time. Its colors stand out flat and positive. They relate it, not to the universal, but to the earth in which it is set. Red Supai sandstone, the rich red rock with the Indian name, the bright red Indian earth that stains land and river alike and give both their name. Green Tonto shale, green as pine and sage, bright as turquoise, clear as the turquoise sky above. Red and green on limestone white. These are its distinctive colours as they are the colors of the old Hopi ceremonial sashes, the masks of the giant Zuñi Shalako, the Navajo blankets, the fine old blankets of Chimayo so faded with their lost and unduplicated colors.

The author FRANK WATER spent much of his childhood in Navajo country, and travelled extensively in the mid-twentieth century in the American Southwest. His descriptive studies of the Grand Canyon is coupled with an understanding of the human character, and the relationship between nature and humanity.

On Snow Peak

Here, on the summit, where the sillness was absolute, unbroken by any sound, and the solitude complete, we thought ourselves beyond the region of animated life; but while we were sitting on the rock, a solitary bee (*Bombus*, the bumblebee) came winging his flight from the eastern valley, and lit on the knee of one of the men.

It was a strange place, the icy rock and the highest peak of the Rocky Mountains, for a lover of warm sunshine and flowers; and we pleased ourselves with the idea that he was the first of his species to cross the mountain barrier – a solitary pioneer to foretell the advance of civilization. I believe that a moment's thought would have made us let him continue his way unharmed; but we carried out the law of this country, where all animated nature seems at war, and, seizing him immediately, put him in at least a fit place – in the leaves of a large book, among the flowers we had collected on our way. The barometer stood at 18.293, the attached thermometer at 44°; giving for the elevation of this summit thirteen thousand five hundred and seventy feet above the Gulf of Mexico, which may be called the highest flight of the bee. It is certainly the highest known flight of that insect.

JOHN CHARLES FREEMONT (1813 – 1890) was the last of the great explorers of the interior of North America, a man who made the unknown countries known. He first crossed the Rocky Mountains in 1842 with Kit Carson as guide; his report of the trip was first published in 1843. Freemont was appointed governor of Arizona Territory in 1878.

The raging waters
and rocky
plateaus of the
Grand Falls on the
Little Colorado
River, a primeval
landscape charac-
terized by the
untamed forces
of nature.

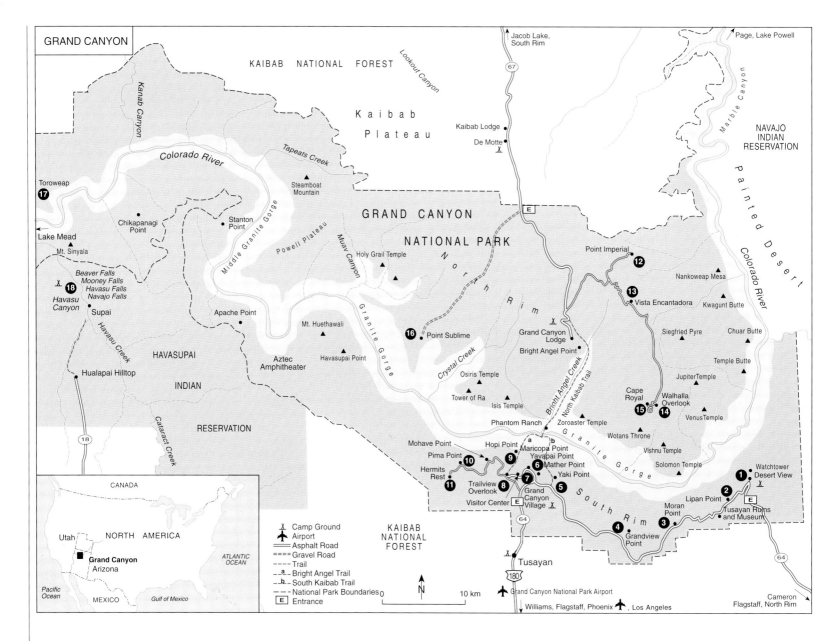

GENERAL INFORMATION

AREA. Grand Canyon National Park, with a surface area of 4,930 square kilometres (1,900 square miles), is the second largest national park in the USA (excluding Alaska) after Yellowstone Park. The park area begins at Lee's Ferry with the Marble Canyon and ends at Grand Wash Cliffs on Lake Mead on the border of Lake Mead National Recreation Area, which is also the border to the state of Nevada. The area from Toroweap lookout point in the west to Little Colorado River, the large tributary of the Colorado in the east, is the most interesting for tourists as well as being the best developed with modern conveniences.

The Grand Canyon is between 6.5 and 29 kilometres (4 and 18 miles) wide. The average width is 14.5 kilometres (9 miles) and the average depth is 1,600 metres (5,250 feet). Mather Point on the South Rim is 1,380 metres (4,500 feet) deep, Grand Canyon Hotel on the North Rim is 1,750 metres (5,750 feet) deep. Mather Point on the South Rim is at a height of 2,130 metres (6,986 feet); the North Rim on the contrary reaches a height of 2,500 metres (8,200 feet). This height difference of 370 metres (1,213 feet) is decisive for the different climatic conditions and consequently for the different vegetation on the North and South Rims. Between Lee's Ferry (950 metres/3,100 feet) and Lake Mead (372 metres/1,220 feet), the Colorado drops 578 metres (1,896 feet), mostly over seventy rapids, which have drops of up to ten metres (32.8 feet).

LOCATION. The Grand Canyon lies in the north of Arizona, which became the 48th State of the United States only in 1912, and which belonged to Mexico as late as 1848. It lies approximately 270 kilometres (168 miles) or a three-hour drive north of the capital city of Phoenix and some 125 kilometres (77.7 miles) north of Flagstaff, a city of 40,000 residents. Geographically, the canyon is part of the Colorado Plateau, covering 377,000 square kilometres (145,900 square miles) in Utah, Colorado, New Mexico and Arizona, just greater than the surface of the Federal Republic of Germany.

HISTORY OF THE NATIONAL PARK.
Impressed by his visit to the Grand Canyon in 1903, American President Theodore Roosevelt arranged the establishment of the Grand Canyon Game Reserve in 1906, and finally had this area declared the Grand Canyon National Monument in 1908. On 26 February 1919, President Woodrow Wilson signed a law in which vast parts of today's park were declared a national park.

In 1922, President Herbert C. Hoover caused the national park to be extended through the addition of a piece of land to the west; in 1969 President Lyndon B. Johnson extended the park to the east of Marble Canyon, which until then had been the eastern border of the park.

Today's park borders were established by President Gerald R. Ford in a law signed on 3 January 1979; certain areas (the adjacent National Monument and parts of Glen Canyon and the Lake Mead Recreation Area) where added but 340 square kilometres (132 square miles) of land were also removed and turned over to the Havasupai Indian Reservation.

INFORMATION

BEFORE LEAVING.
Arizona Office of Tourism
1100 West Washington, Phoenix, Arizona 85007 (tel: 602-542-4003, fax 602-542-4068).

Superintendent Grand Canyon National Park
P.O. Box 129
Grand Canyon, Arizona 86023
(tel: 602-638-7888).
The hiking permits required for the descent and overnight stay in the canyon can be obtained here.

Above: The line to the Grand Canyon was inaugurated in 1901; before this, tourists travelled to the canyon on horseback. Below: Mine-owner William W. Bass (photo right) organized trips to the canyon beginning in 1890, and is considered to be one of the founders of tourism in the region.

ON THE SPOT. Everything one needs to know about the Grand Canyon can be discovered in the Visitors' Center in Grand Canyon Village (South Rim). Here, there are wall charts, geological and topographical maps and literature of all types as well as talks, slide and film presentations. The *Yavapai Point Museum*, in the immediate vicinity, offers interesting displays of the canyon's geology and a splendid view of the canyon from the picture window. On the North Rim as well there is a small information centre in the foyer of the Grand Canyon Hotel.

Tips on excursions and hikes in more remote areas and off the much trodden paths are provided by the *Bureau of Land Management (BLM)*. This public authority is responsible for the administration of unused public land which belongs to the State. The branch office in Utah is the competent authority for the Grand Canyon surroundings and, consequently, areas in Utah such as Paria Canyon, Buckskin Gulch and Grand Gulch Primitive Area:

Kanab Resource Area,
918 North East, Kanab, Utah 84741.

HOW TO GET THERE

The ideal way to visit the Grand Canyon is to "Fly and Drive" with a car or camper rented (and paid for in advance) at home, as it is cheaper. It is important to pay attention to "unlimited mileage" at the time of rental; this means that all mileage is included in the basic price (without gas). The country is big and it is annoying to be obliged to think about the additional costs for every trip or every detour.

Travel agencies offer cars in five sizes, as well as a large selection of motor homes, from camping buses up to ten-metre-long (30 foot-long) units. All the necessary details and price lists are found in the agency brochures.

The choice of airport depends upon which sights in addition to the Grand Canyon are on the itinerary. The decision to rent a vehicle after arrival is also a determining factor; for example, mobile homes can only be rented in larger cities.

The closest city airport to the Grand Canyon is Phoenix, Arizona, which, however, cannot be reached non-stop by air from Europe. Changing in an American airport is relatively involved; after the first landing in the USA, the luggage must be brought

Above: A viewpoint with a mineral shop: "Lookout Studio" in Grand Canyon Village.
Below: The nostalgic railway between Williams and Grand Canyon Village.

through customs and then checked in anew. The tiny Grand Canyon National Park Airport is just a few kilometres away from the south entrance of the park.

Because the driving time from Los Angeles to Phoenix is now only six hours, since the speed limit was raised from 55 to 65 miles an hour (from 90 to 110 kilometres per hour) on the interstate highways, Los Angeles is definitely worth considering as an alternative for an arrival airport and a place to spend the first night.

Most Europeans now require only a passport for entry into the country. Those who have already visited the United States and therefore still have a visa (formerly valid

for a lifetime) should bring it with them, even if the passport has expired; the visa is still valid and facilitates the entry formalities. European cash is not well known in the United States and is therefore usually not exchanged.

In addition to a few dollars for the first few days after landing, it is therefore recommended to have traveller's cheques in US dollars (they can be used like cash) and, this applies for the entire journey, a major credit card (Visa, Eurocard/Master Card or American Express). Travellers who do not possess such a card may be considered untrustworthy clients and consequently would pay hotel costs in advance or pay a

In Grand Canyon Village, directly on the edge of the abyss, are the famous Hotel El Tovar (above) and Hopi House (below), in which Indian arts and crafts are sold.

closed from the end of November to the middle of May. Its own loose gravel road leads to the Toroweap lookout point on the North Rim of the canyon. For visitors who do not intend to descend into the abyss, every season is suitable; however, notice must be taken of the winter closing of the North Rim.

It is otherwise for those who wish to go down the river. In summer, temperatures can be expected to go up to 48 degrees Celsius (118 degrees Fahrenheit). There-fore, spring and fall are best for hiking.

For those who can manage it, it is best to avoid a visit to the canyon during Amer-ican school holidays from mid-June until the beginning of September. The influx during this period is at its greatest and no accommodation can be obtained without reservations made well in advance. The same applies for important American holi-days such as the period around Memorial Day, which falls on the last Monday in May. The entry price to the national park is charged according to car or mobile home, independent of the number of passen-gers. The entrance ticket allows as many park entries as desired for one week. Those who wish to visit other national parks or national monuments during their holidays in the USA should obtain the Golden Eagle Pass, which allows multiple entries into these areas for an entire calen-dar year.

ACCOMMODATION

HOTELS. Hotels and lodges on the South Rim are operated by the Grand Canyon Na-tional Park Lodges (Fred Harvey Company, P.O. Box 699, Grand Canyon, Arizona 86 023); the *Grand Canyon Lodge* on the North Rim is operated by the Grand Can-yon Lodge TW Recreational Services (P.O. Box 400, Cedar City, Utah 84 720).

Room reservations by telephone can only be made by those in possession of major credit cards. Issuing company (Master Card, Visa, American Express, etc.) and card number as well as expiration date must be stated when making the reserva-tion. Those who intend to arrive late (after six in the evening) must expressly request a guaranteed reservation. The room is then held the whole night.

All the hotels on the South Rim are in Grand Canyon Village. As elsewhere in the USA, all the rooms are air-conditioned and have television. Next to the canyon are the

higher deposit when renting a car. And as credit cards can be used in most every shop and restaurant in the United States, they are worth having along in any case.

From Phoenix, it is 145 car kilometres (90 miles, about 1.5 hours' driving time) on Interstate 17 to Flagstaff and an additional 125 kilometres (77 miles, another 1.5 driv-ing hours) to Grand Canyon Village on the South Rim.

From Flagstaff, there is a year-round bus connection to the park. In addition, since 1989 a nostalgic railway pulled by a steam engine has been running on the historical railway line from Williams to Grand Can-yon Village.

TRAVEL SEASONS AND POINTS OF ACCESS

Grand Canyon National Park has three en-trances. On the South Rim, one arrives at Grand Canyon Village and Desert View; on the North Rim there is a road over Jacob Lake. Between the North Rim and the South Rim there are only 16 kilometres (10 miles) as the crow flies or a steep 33 kilometre (20 mile) hiking path, but this is an equivalent to 345 car kilometres (215 miles) or five hours' driving time.

The South Rim is accessible all year round; however, the entrance to the North Rim is

El Tovar (the best place in town), *Kachina Lodge, Thunderbird Lodge* and *Bright Angel Lodge* hotels, which also have cabins. Be careful when making a reservation: not every room has a view of the canyon, even in "the best hotels".

The other hotels on the South Rim, *Old* and *New Yavapai Lodge, Motor Lodge* and *Maswik Lodge*, are set back a little, and therefore rooms with a view cannot be expected. *The Phantom Ranch* on the north bank of the Colorado beyond the Kaibab Suspension Bridge is a special place, for it offers dormitories and cabins for up to four people; accommodation and meals must be reserved in advance.

Outside the park there are a few hotels, motels and lodges, just ten kilometres (6.2

Hotel; two others, *Mather Campground* and *Trailer Village* (especially designed for camping vehicles) in Grand Canyon Village; and one near *Desert View*, on the South Rim. It is not possible to reserve places in the Desert View campground; it is therefore recommended to be there early in the day.

It is possible and recommended to reserve for the other places through a central reservation agency: Ticketron, P.O. Box 62429, Virginia Beach, Virginia 23462. There are showers on the North Rim and in Grand Canyon Village.

There are simple campgrounds outside the park (without electricity, water and waste-water connections) in *De Motte* and *Jacob Lake* in *Tusayan (Ten-X)*.

ACTIVITIES

Circled numbers refer to the map on page 48; those in italics refer to the colour photographs.

From the peaceful contemplation of the changing play of light and colour from one of the lookout points at sunrise and sunset to the athletic crossing of the canyon on foot, there is much to see and do in the canyon. Information concerning planned events can be obtained in the Visitors' Center. The programme can also be obtained by writing to the National Park Service, P.O. Box 129, Grand Canyon, Arizona 86023.

More than four million visitors come to the Grand Canyon yearly. Ninety percent limit themselves to a sightseeing tour along the canyon's rim. The interior of the canyon can scarcely cope with more than the remaining ten percent, currently around 400,000 hikers, riders and rubber dinghy operators.

HIKING. Of the total of nineteen footpaths in the canyon, only *Bright Angel Trail* and *Kaibab Trail* are permanently maintained by the park administration.

The Bright Angel Trail starts in Grand Canyon Village and runs along 12.5 kilometres (7.7 miles) to the 1,370-metre (4,494-foot) lower Phantom Ranch on the north bank of the Colorado, which one crosses on the Kaibab Suspension Bridge built in 1907. *9*

The steeper Kaibab Trail begins at Yaki Point, approximately seven kilometres (4.35 miles) east of Grand Canyon Village, and reaches the 1,460-metre (4,789-foot) lower suspension bridge after just over eleven kilometres (6.8 miles). It continues for twenty-two kilometres (13.7 miles) to Grand Canyon Lodge on the North Rim, at a height of 1,750 metres (5,740 feet). This is the only path crossing the canyon. *16/17, 23, 24, 25, 27*

The *Rim Trail* is equally extensive. It runs 14.5 kilometres (9 miles) along the canyon from Yavapi Point on the South Rim to Hermit's Rest. The *Widforss Trail* on the North Rim is almost level, running for eight kilometres (five miles) through the woods, along a side canyon called a transept, to Widforss Point (2,403 metres/7,882 feet), from where one can look into the main canyon. No hiking permit is required for this trail.

Phantom Ranch on the Colorado River, an overnight stop for those crossing the canyon.

miles) south of the park's entrance in Tusayan, Arizona 86023: the *Moqui Lodge* (Fred Harvey Company, see address above), the *Quality Inn* (P.O. Box 520) and the *Best Western Grand Canyon Squire Inn* (P.O. Box 130).

If all the rooms on the canyon's rim are reserved, it is then possible in an emergency to give the *Cameron Trading Post Motel* in Cameron a try (tel: 602-679-2231). Otherwise it is necessary to go to Williams or Flagstaff, 90 and 125 kilometres (56 and 77 miles) respectively from the Grand Canyon.

CAMPING. There are four campgrounds in the Grand Canyon National Park: one on the North Rim near the Grand Canyon

FOOD AND DRINK

There are no gourmet restaurants in the Grand Canyon area, but most of the hotels mentioned have restaurants with simple and hearty cooking.

One can eat well in the tasteful atmosphere of the elegant *Hotel El Tovar*. Cafeterias and snack-bars can be found in Grand Canyon Village, in Desert View and in Hermit's Rest.

Many visitors prefer to make their own lunch in one of the numerous picnic grounds which offer shaded tables and benches as well as wonderful scenery. For those who decide on this option, there are good shopping possibilities in Mather Shopping Center in Grand Canyon Village.

A hike down into the canyon is the best way to discover its flora and fauna, its history and characteristics. When planning such a tour, a few important points should be taken into consideration.

It is better to start the canyon crossing on the North Rim, because there is an approximate 400 metre (1,300 feet) difference in height involved in the ascent to the South Rim than in the opposite direction. In addition to excellent physical condition, this undertaking requires a certain amount of organization, for from the North Rim to the South Rim there are only 33 kilometres (20 miles) of footpath, but there is an equivalent of 345 car kilometres (215 miles) to be covered. Because there is no regular bus connection between the two points, a companion with a car is needed to return to the starting point of the hike.

The North Kaibab Trail runs from the North Rim down into the canyon for approximately 22 kilometres (14 miles). The night can be spent in the Phantom Ranch or at Bright Angel Campground. A word of caution: accommodation in the Phantom Ranch should be reserved at least six months in advance. For every hike including an overnight stay in the canyon, a hiking permit is required, which one is well advised to procure some three to six months prior to the hike. For most visitors to the canyon, the South Rim is both the starting and finishing point of a hike. Two permanently maintained paths run from here down into the abyss, the advantages and disadvantages of which must be weighed against each other.

The Bright Angel Trail begins in centrally located Grand Canyon Village. Long-term parking is also available here. With an average width of one and-a-half metres (five feet), the Bright Angel Trail is better developed than the second path, the Kaibab Trail. And although it is 12.5 kilometres (7.8 miles) longer, there are almost 100 fewer metres of height difference (328 feet) to be overcome up to the Kaibab Suspension Bridge: the Bright Angel Trail is therefore less steep than the Kaibab Trail. Indeed, the trail is used by the mule trains precisely for this reason. An encounter with them can be particularly unpleasant when this takes place on a part of the path cut into the steep cliffs. In this case the rule applies that the animals are

ON THE MOVE
IN THE CANYON

Kaibab Suspension Bridge.

On the steep South Kaibab Trail hikers find neither shade nor water.

permitted to remain close to the mountainside. The hiker must continue directly along the edge, hoping that one of the mules will not suddenly take a step to the side!

It is usually recommended to take the steep, dry Kaibab Trail for the descent, and to follow the Bright Angel Trail on the return trip where there is shade and water available.

How much time should one plan for the trip down and back or for crossing the canyon? It depends entirely on your condition: the record time for crossing the canyon on the Kaibab Trail was four hours, an almost inconceivable achievement for thirty-tree kilometres (twenty miles) and a total height difference of 3,210 metres (10,530 feet).

Well-trained hikers, if they leave early enough, can manage the trip down to the river and back in one day. But this leaves little time for lingering or catching one's breath, looking at the magnificent scenery or wildlife along the way, or for taking photographs. It is better to spread the trip there and back over a more leisurely-paced two to four days.

Bivouac sites are available at the half-way mark. One must remember that a desert climate prevails on the canyon floor, so a warm sweater is a not-to-be-forgotten necessity. In addition to appropriate shoes and a good map, headgear and adequately large water bottles are also a necessary part of the equipment.

Though somewhat strenuous, the descent into the canyon is worth the effort: it is one of life's experiences which remain engraved in the memory.

Helmut Friedrich

Mule excursions in the Grand Canyon. The return trip is usually made on the Bright Angel Trail (below), and on the Kaibab Trail for two-day excursions (above).

For the particularly ambitious hiker, there is *Tonto Trail*, a 115 kilometre (71 mile) trail up to the Tonto Plateau above the Inner Gorge, on which there is neither shade nor water! Information on this and other paths can be obtained free of charge at the Backcountry Reservation Office, P.O. Box 129, Grand Canyon, Arizona 86023. All hikers wishing to descend into the canyon and spend the night require a hiking permit which is granted free of charge in the Backcountry Reservation Office, but it is only made available to those whose equipment meets their requirements. The size of the water bottles is of particular interest: the absolute minimum is a reserve of four litres (one gallon) per person. It is important to know that a person can expend up to eight litres (two gallons) of water per day in the dry heat of the canyon.

Rangers are authorized to refuse hiking permits to persons whose constitution does not appear to them to be suitable. Apparently, however, the park guards are quite generous in their evaluation of the tourists' physical state, for all too often exhausted hikers call for their help.

Help comes in the shape of two mules and one mule guide. The "rescue" is undertaken, however, only after payment in advance, due to bad experiences with victims allegedly unable to pay. Faced with the alternative of being left, there are very rarely problems with paying up. It is obvious that such a rescue operation is expensive. It would be even more expensive to fly out with a helicopter, which is only authorized in serious cases of emergency requiring swift medical treatment. The trails which are no longer maintained can be very dangerous in parts: hikers wishing to go on these trails must prove that they have already followed Bright Angel Trail or Kaibab Trail. They must also leave an exact timetable of their hike and provide the exact hour of their return. These trails are fascinating for the experienced hiker who already knows the canyon well, for they offer a profusion of new impressions. Some run past open copper, silver, asbestos, lead and platinum mines, none of which was ever profitable; and no wonder, with the laborious and costly ore transportation out of the canyon. Only bat-guano mining in a gigantic cave in the west of the Grand Canyon was fairly profitable, and for this one of the longest cable railways of the world was built.

RIDING. Riding is undeniably less strenuous than walking, but one must not imagine that a ride into the canyon is easy. Many a rider has preferred to descend into the canyon on foot.

The bridle-path, the Bright Angel Trail, runs close to appalling abysses at times. Riders suffering from dizziness must occasionally have sacks placed over their heads in these areas and must be tightly bound to their animals.

It is important to know that the riding order within the caravan cannot be changed and the train can stop only upon the appropriate signal by the caravan leader. The riders must be at least twelve years old, must not weigh more than ninety kilograms (two hundred pounds) and not have more than five kilograms (eleven pounds) of luggage with them, including photographic equipment. Excursions from two hours to three days are offered. The sole company to offer these services is the Fred Harvey Company, P.O. Box 699, Grand Canyon, Arizona 86023. Reservations should be made a year in advance, if possible.

Mule rides in the canyon are also offered from the North Rim. Reservations for these not so popular tours can be made at the Grand Canyon Lodge.

CLIMBING. The Grand Canyon also offers good climbing possibilities, as, for example, the isolated rising Vishnu Butte and the Zoroaster Temple. Climbing tours are in the domain of backcountry trips. Before commencing such an undertaking, a detailed discussion of one's intentions with the park officials is required, in order to obtain the indispensable authorization.

BOAT TRIPS. A rubber dinghy boat trip on the Colorado is a special experience. It is less arduous than a ride or a hike (one is only shaken up in the ten-metre/thirty-foot rapids) and offers an incomparable landscape experience: the trips in the unsinkable rubber boats offer the only way to see the Inner Gorge close up, that section of the canyon in which the Colorado has dug deeply into the hard Vishnu slate (two-billion-year-old rock).

Regulations call for the wearing of a life vest, which is not a very tempting prospect in the narrow, crowded boats and the canyon's summer temperatures. But thanks to these safety measures there have been no deaths since commercialized boating began, despite some capsizings.

Because the big rubber dinghies are driven by out-board motors, and several boats follow behind one another, all occupants except for those in the first boat must swallow some exhaust fumes. But this only slightly affects the enjoyment of the scenery; in any case one gets extremely wet on such a trip. In addition to rubber dinghy trips, trips in simple row-boats are also offered, from one-day excursions to ten-day trips from Lee's Ferry to Lake Mead.

Information and reservations: Fred Harvey Transportation Company, P.O. Box 709, Grand Canyon, Arizona 86023.

The trip from Lee's Ferry to Lake Mead is so popular that it is again necessary to make reservations one year in advance. The number of boat tourists is limited to fifty thousand per year, which implies that the reservation deadline will become longer as the number of visitors continues to rise.

SIGHTSEEING FLIGHTS. One can get to know the Grand Canyon from a different but also very exciting perspective by taking a sightseeing flight above the gorge. Flights through the canyon ("under the rim") have unfortunately been prohibited in recent years following some tragic acci-

Above: The canyon landscape is particularly impressive when seen during a boat trip.
Below: The Colorado presents a challenge even to the well-trained kayaker.

dents, including collisions between propeller-driven airplanes and helicopters. These truly breath-taking flights can, however, still be experienced as in real life on a giant screen in the IMAX cinema in Tusayan.

Flights for groups and individuals in propeller-driven airplanes and helicopters (all with good views) are offered from Las Vegas, Phoenix (Scottsdale), Page and Tusayan.

Reservations: Scenic Airlines, Las Vegas, Nevada, or Scottsdale, Arizona; Lake Powell Air, Page, Arizona; Grand Canyon Airlines and Grand Canyon Helicopters, both in Tusayan, Arizona.

VIEWPOINTS AND POINTS OF INTEREST

SOUTH RIM. The South Rim of the canyon can be reached from Williams or Flagstaff, from Grand Canyon Village, from Page, or from Flagstaff, on State Highway 64, with a small detour over Cameron.

It is recommended to begin the sightseeing tour at Desert View in the southeast region of the canyon, and to follow a route which runs along the canyon rim. Thus, one starts with one of the most attractive views of the canyon and the Colorado, which is often no longer visible during the course of the journey, reaching the large and hectic Grand Canyon Village later on. (It is convenient that one is already on the "right side" of the road, so that for all the following sights, one need only turn right).

Between Desert View at the start of East Rim Drive and Hermit's Rest at the end of West Rim, there are eleven additional "official" lookout points, all worth visiting. They will be briefly described in order of their appearance along this stretch of road. *2, 6/7, 19, 29, 31, 44/45*

The Watchtower at Desert View.

Desert View ①. There is a grandiose view the length of the canyon from the *Watchtower*, a lookout tower of some 20 metres (65 feet) in height.

The tower is admittedly not a historical structure built by Indians – it was erected only in 1932 – but it is modelled on the old Indian protective formations and camps. Inside, there is an exposition of Indian arts and crafts, which are also offered for sale. *4/5*

Lipan Point ②, the nearest lookout point on the East Rim Drive, offers a particularly beautiful view into the eastern part of the canyon.

In the nearby *Tusayan Museum* there are numerous finds from old Indian cultures of the region. Not far from the museum there is an uncovered pueblo of the Anasazi Indians, the former inhabitants of the Colorado Plateau, dating from the twelfth century.

Particularly attractive views of the Grand Canyon and the Colorado River are furnished by the Moran Point (above) and Lipan Point (below) lookouts.

Moran Point ③. From here the *Hance Rapids*, the rapids of the Colorado with a ten-metre (30-foot) drop are visible.

Grandview Point ④ reveals perhaps the most attractive view from the South Rim.

Yaki Point ⑤. From this lookout, the dark *Granite Gorge*, also called *Inner Gorge*, is visible. This is the lowest point of the canyon; here the Colorado has dug deeply into two billion-year-old rock, the Vishnu slate. There is a good view from here of the *Kaibab Trail* and *Bright Angel Trail* in the distance.

Mather Point ⑥ is the first lookout which the visitor reaches on coming into the Grand Canyon National Park through the south entrance. If one looks closely, one can even see the *Bright Angel Trail* from here as well as the *Phantom Ranch* on Bright Angel Creek. *3*

Yavapai Point ⑥, as does Mather Point in the immediate vicinity of the *Grand Canyon Village* ⑦, offers one of the classical views of the canyon. Here are found the above-mentioned *Yavapai Point Museum* and the *Visitors' Center*. The museum, which is decidedly worth seeing, is par-

Each lookout point offers visitors fascinating new perspectives of the Grand Canyon: Yaki Point (above) and Mather Point (below).

ticularly devoted to the creation, erosion and geology of the canyon.

After busy Grand Canyon Village, the main town on the South Rim, the West Rim Drive runs further along the canyon, although it is closed to private cars during the high season. A free commuter bus drives along the stretch from the Bright Angel Lodge to the end of the road, Hermit's Rest, stopping at every official lookout.

Trailview Overlook ⑧. Here one's gaze falls onto the *Bright Angel Trail*, with its cheerfully descending hikers and its tired hikers trudging back up.

Maricopa Point ⑨. There is a good view from here of the west part of the canyon. Not too far away, on *Powell Point*, there is a *memorial to Major John Wesley Powell*, explorer of the Colorado.

If sunset is approaching, it is not worth lingering here: though the scenery is good, it is best to be out of the area before dark. *37*

Hopi Point ⑨, the next lookout point, which projects deep into the canyon, is amongst the best places to observe the fascinating play of colours at sunrise and sunset. *36*

Mohave Point ⑩. The road runs behind this lookout point to *The Abyss*, a place which plunges nearly 900 metres (3,000 feet) vertically into the depths.

Pima Point ⑩ offers a view of the undulating course of the Colorado. When all is quiet here, one can hear the roar of the notorious *Granite Rapids*.

Hermit's Rest ⑪ marks the end of the road. It is so called because a French-Canadian hermit lived here for twenty years.

Bright Angel Creek near Phantom Ranch.

Today there is a souvenir stand and a snack-bar on the spot.

NORTH RIM. Only ten percent of the park's visitors make it to the canyon's North Rim. Perhaps this is due to the fact that from Los Angeles or Phoenix it is some 350 kilometres (217 miles) longer than the way to the South Rim. Or perhaps the rumour has been spread that the view of the canyon from here is less impressive than on the opposite side. Indeed, the Colorado is further away from the North Rim and cannot be seen as well as from the South Rim.

On the other hand, isolated and tranquil places can be found on the North Rim, places which are almost non-existent on the South Rim. *32/33*

One can reach the North Rim via Kanab, Utah, or Page, Arizona, over Highway 89 which joins Highway 67 at Jacob Lake. This stretch ends at the *Grand Canyon Lodge*,

A view from Hopi Point: deeply fissured terrain as far as the eye can see.

Toroweap ⑰. Similar to Havasu Canyon, this area, sometimes called Tuweep Canyon, on the North Rim of the Grand Canyon can be reached only after a long drive on an unpaved road. Three roads will take you there, from Fredonia, Arizona (105 kilometres/65 miles), two hours; from St. George, Utah (145 kilometres/90 miles), three hours; and from Colorado City, Arizona (90 kilometres/56 miles). Because the last road is usually in poor repair, it is not possible to provide a quote on the time spent travelling. The route from Fredonia, which branches off from Highway 389 west of Fredonia to the south, is recommended. The view from Toroweap Overlook is unique in the Grand Canyon. There is a sheer drop from the rock face down to the Colorado, which roars 900 metres (2,952 feet) below and which overlooks the river for kilometres. The Lava Falls Rapids can be seen; they are amongst the most dangerous rapids in the Grand Canyon. Also visible are lava remnants from the time of lively volcanic activity in the canyon approximately one million years ago. High dams were formed by the lava streams pouring into the canyon, one of which dammed the Colorado for over 300 kilometres (186 miles).

A word of caution: As there are no railings along the vertically plunging rock face, visitors who tend to dizzy spells on heights are advised not to approach the chasm too closely. At the lookout point there is a small camping ground on which, however, there are no services, meaning no water. But it is worth a visit: the façade glows a deep red at sunrise, while the river is swathed in mysterious darkness. Around ten o'clock in the morning, one can see the large rubber dinghies of the Colorado expeditions to Lava Falls dance over the waves.

HAVASU CANYON ⑱. Although it is no longer situated within the boundaries of the national park, Havasu Canyon, a remarkably beautiful side canyon of the Colorado, is part of the Grand Canyon, and is of particular interest to tourists. The canyon conceals a green oasis in the midst of rocky terrain.

Those prepared to spare no expense and who reserve long enough in advance can fly in a helicopter from Tusayan to *Supai*, the little village in the Havasu Canyon. Riders and hikers – motorists and even bicycles are prohibited – must book their

the only hotel on the North Rim. A few kilometres from this spot, the road branches to the left to the lookouts *Point Imperial* ⑫, which is situated on a sideroad, *Vista Encantadora*⑬, *Walhalla Overlook* ⑭ and *Cape Royal*.

Cape Royal ⑮ probably offers the most impressive view from the North Rim. The footpath, scarcely one kilometre (a little over half a mile) long, from the parking lot to the lookout, runs past *Angel's Window*, a stone bridge through which one can see the Colorado River as if looking through a window in the rocks.

In the foreground tower majestic buttes with equally illustrious names such as Vishnu Temple, Wotan's Throne, the more-distant Solomon Temple and Venus Temple, and Zoroaster Temple. The view extends to Navajo Mountain.

Point Sublime ⑯. Just before the branch-off to the four lookout points here there is a gravel road to the right, an excursion worth taking but for which it is necessary to plan enough time: the drive there and back on the approximately thirty kilometre (nineteen mile) track requires almost half a day to drive.

animals and accommodation in advance: Havasupai Tourist Enterprise, Supai, Arizona; Havasupai Lodges, Supai, Arizona.

The first part of the journey is undertaken by car: from Flagstaff one hundred-twenty kilometres (seventy-five miles) on the I-40 to Seligman, then forty kilometres (twenty-five miles) on the historical route 66 to the Grand Canyon Caverns, where there is the last gas station, and shortly after that along road 18, which is paved all the way, for one hundred kilometres

An Indian settlement in Havasu Canyon.

(sixty-two miles) north to the end of this road, which is called *Hualapai Hilltop*, 1,585 metres (5,200 feet) above sea-level. Here, at the car terminus, the real tour begins. A trail pass must be obtained to visit the Havasu Canyon. There are twelve kilometres (7.5 miles) to be done on foot, mule or horse before reaching the village of Supai, 800 metres (2,625 feet) below.

Visitors can spend the night here in a sleeping bag or tent which has been brought along, but there is also a perfectly comfortable twenty-four room hotel accommodating up to four people in each room. Advance reservations are highly recommended.

There is also a so-called "eatery" in Supai, a cafeteria in which Indian meals are offered in addition to the obligatory hamburgers. Note: the cafeteria closes in the evening at 7:00 pm. As in all Indian reservations across America, there is a strict ban on alcohol; bringing and consuming it is therefore not allowed. Below Supai are the waterfalls which have made the canyon

Above: From Imperial Point on the North Rim, one's gaze falls on the mighty plateau.
Below: A view from Toroweap Overlook into the depths.

famous: *Navajo Falls, Havasu Falls, Mooney Falls* and *Beaver Falls*. Below Beaver Falls the path is at times steep, slippery and narrow; good shoes are required for this stage of the journey. From the last of the waterfalls, Beaver Falls, it is only five kilometres (three miles) to the Havasu Creek estuary in the Colorado. The path ends here. *38, 39*

EXCURSIONS

Those who undertake the long flight to the west of the USA will not wish to limit their sightseeing programme to the Grand Can-yon; rather, they will wish to visit it as part of a round trip. The small towns of Flagstaff and Page offer good bases for interesting day excursions.

DAY TRIP DESTINATIONS FROM FLAGSTAFF. Diamond Creek. In Peach Springs on the I-40, a gravel road – Diamond Creek Road – branches to the north. It ends after approximately thirty kilometres (twenty miles) at *Diamond Point*. Formerly the site of a simple hotel which burned down in 1914, Diamond Point today is just one of the destinations on the banks of the Colorado which can be reached by car, a place on the Hualapai Indian Reservation in which one can find isolation and tranquility. There is a (small) toll for the road; it is advisable to inquire beforehand as to the current state of the road in Peach Springs.

Lee's Ferry. At Lee's Ferry there is an exceptional possibility of reaching the banks of the Colorado by car. At this point, where today's Grand Canyon National Park begins, John D. Lee, an outlaw of the Mormon Wars, established a ferry over the Colorado, originally with the discarded boats from the Powell Expedition. This is where the Colorado rubber dinghy expeditions start today. In the immediate surroundings gigantic mushroom-shaped stones can be found. The filigree *Navajo Bridge* over the Colorado is also worth seeing; all those who wish to travel from one rim of the canyon to the other must pass over it.

Meteor Crater. In Winslow, approximately eighty kilometres (fifty miles) east of Flagstaff, south of I-40, lies one of the largest and best-preserved meteor craters of the world. Some 22,000 years ago a 60,000-ton nickel-iron meteor struck at a speed of approximately 45,000 kilometres (28,000 miles) per hour. It is estimated that 500 million tons of rocks were hurled aloft. The crater's diameter measures 1,265 metres (4,150 feet) and is 175 metres (575 feet) deep.

Oak Creek Canyon. Highway ALT 89 runs forty kilometres (twenty-five miles) to the south of Flagstaff through a romantic valley with numerous lakes and rivers, coniferous trees and red rocks. In the centre of the valley is the *Sedona* artists' colony.

Petrified Forest National Park. This national park is part of the Painted Desert area of the Mojave Desert, the peripheral field of which can be seen from Desert View on the South Rim. Here are coloured clay hills, in which lie the greatest number of petrified tree trunks known to the world, and often still completely preserved. The trunks are approximately 200 million years old. Over the course of time, the organic material of the trunks which fell into the swamp, to be later covered with mud, was replaced by silicic acid, which formed minute quartz crystals in the wood's cells.

Above: Gigantic mushroom-shaped stone formations near Lee's Ferry.
Below: Tree stumps approximately 200 million years old in Petrified Forest National Park.

Many of the petrified trees belong as Araucaria to the coniferous group. Distant relations of the Araucaria still grow today, as the Araucarioxyla in South America, Australia and New Zealand. The Petrified Forest lies directly on the I-40, approximately 150 kilometres (93 miles) to the east of Flagstaff.

Walnut Canyon National Monument, close to the I-40, is some fifteen kilometres (nine miles) to the east of Flagstaff, practically within the city limits. Over three hundred Sinagua Indian pueblos from the twelfth and thirteenth centuries can be

seen here below the steep jutting rock. The lookout points can be reached easily by paved roads.

Wupatki National Monument. On an eastern branch road of Highway 89 between Flagstaff and Grand Canyon is a centuries-old Indian settlement. Here are the remains of the Anasazi pueblos from the pre-Columbian period (twelfth and thirteenth centuries), as well as multi-storied buildings and a ball-playing field, which puzzled architects for a long time. The fertile ashes spewed by the nearby Sunset Volcano in *Sunset Crater* (also an interest-

Above: A tranquil trip in a houseboat on Lake Powell.
Below: The ruins of one of the more than 800 prehistoric Wupatki National Monument edifices.

ing excursion) once provided favourable conditions for establishing a settlement.

DAY TRIP DESTINATIONS FROM PAGE. Lake Powell.

The lake created by the damming of the Colorado flooded the hitherto almost unknown Glen Canyon. With a surface of 660 square kilometres (255 square miles) and a perimeter of 3,140 kilometres (1,950 miles), it is one of the largest artificial lakes in the world. In addition to its intended purpose - regulation and energy exploitation of the Colorado - Lake Powell is an increasingly popular playground for motor-boats and

houseboats of all sizes. Page, a former construction workers' settlement a few kilometres away from the lake, is a first-rate tourist centre today. There are five large marinas on the lake: Wahweap, Dangling Rope, Bullfrog, Hite and Hall's Crossing, where boats can be rented.

The most peaceful and relaxing way to discover Lake Powell with its ninety-six side canyons is most certainly to travel it with a houseboat. It is wise to reserve at least a year in advance for the high season (July to the beginning of September).

Houseboats are slow, with little draught, and are therefore very sensitive to the high

waves caused by fast boats. With a common room, several bedrooms, showers, refrigerator, television and air-conditioning, houseboats offer every comfort. Depending on the size of the boat, they can sleep six, ten or twelve people. No special license is required to pilot the boat, the hirers are satisfied with providing quick instructions.

A houseboat should be rented for at least a week. Those not wishing to devote quite so much time to Lake Powell can travel in four hours there and back to *Rainbow Bridge* eighty kilometres (fifty miles) away on a half-day tour from Wahweap Marina in a 1,600 hp speedboat.

These tours are also available as day trips and offer, in addition to Rainbow Bridge (the stop there is one hour, but only thirty minutes on the half-day trip), detours into alarmingly narrow, exceedingly attractive side canyons. The captains enjoy piloting the boats deep into the narrow canyons until they grind against the steep rock façades, alarming the passengers.

Only a few sites on the banks of Lake Powell can be reached by car – not even all the above-mentioned marinas: Dangling Rope Marina is only accessible by sea. Sightseeing flights over Lake Powell are obtainable in Page. They are also interesting because one can see the buttes in the lake, from whose small, vertically dropping plateaus numerous automobiles occupied by villains have been tossed in movies and commercials. Information: National Park Service, Glen Canyon Recreation Area, P.O. Box 1507, Page, Arizona 860 40, and Carl Hayden Visitors' Center, directly on Glen Canyon Dam, as well as at the Bullfrog Marina.

Hotel, Houseboat and Excursion Reservations: Lake Powell Resorts & Marinas ARA Leisure Services, 2916 N. 35th Avenue, Suite 8, Phoenix, Arizona 85017-5261.
40/41

Monument Valley Navajo Tribal Park.

Within the Navajo Indian Reservation, partly in Utah, but mostly in Arizona, approximately 180 kilometres (110 miles) east of Page, lies Monument Valley, which became world-famous as the setting of many westerns. A gravel road, open to drivers of private cars, runs through Monument Valley; the round-trip is approximately 28 kilometres (18 miles). Another gravel road round-trip, equally long, is possible only with a driver and an

A RAINBOW TURNED TO STONE

Though it would be futile to argue about which is the most beautiful of the natural wonders created by the Colorado River and its tributaries, the uniqueness of Rainbow Bridge cannot be denied.

For the Navajo, Ute, and Paiute Indians, the "Nonnezoshi", the rainbow of stone, is an object of particular veneration. For them, it is a guardian, a keeper of the almighty universe. The largest and most attractive natural stone bridge in the world – its span is eighty-four metres (275 feet), its height eighty-eight metres (289 feet), its width almost ten metres (thirty-three feet) at its highest point – was not "discovered" by the Whites until 1909.

Two expeditions set off that year, quite by chance at the same time: one was directed by Byron Cummings, an archaeologist from the University of Utah, and John Wetherhill, owner of a business near Oljeto, Arizona with Nasja Begay of the Paiute tribe acting as guide); the other was led by William Douglass with Jim Mike of the Ute tribe as a guide. By chance, the groups heard of each another, joined forces, and after a strenuous and dangerous ride reached the Rainbow Bridge together on 14 August 1909.

The end of the expedition turned into a farce. Douglass was determined to be the first to ride over the bridge, but did not see it right away. Wetherhill had better eyes, spurred his horse on, passing Douglass, and proclaimed himself the dis-

Above and below: A former Indian place of worship, the majestic Rainbow Bridge.

coverer of the bridge. A fight also erupted between the two Indian guides about which one of them had actually led the expedition to the bridge.

One year later, the Rainbow Bridge was declared a national monument by then President William H. Taft, giving it the conservation status as well as the national recognition it truly deserves.

Geologists differentiate between "arches", formed by erosion without the effect of water, and "bridges", formed by flowing water carrying sediment. As the name suggests, Rainbow Bridge should be classified with the bridges.

Its formation is thought to be thus: before the Colorado Plateau began to rise approximately sixty million years ago, the rivers meandered in the lowlands. When the terrain rose, their course was accelerated, digging more deeply into the earth. This caused the grinding of a rock façade which had separated two river bends to such an extent that it broke in two: the river carved out a new bed, enlarging the breakthrough point, causing the formation of a rocky bridge connecting the two shores.

An important condition for the formation of the Rainbow Bridge was the texture of the so-called Navajo sandstone, a brittle, porous rock which tends to flake. As part of this same group, the gigantic grottoes near Rainbow Bridge and the arches in Arches National Park owe their existence to this same property.

When examined from this more scientific point of view, the conditions for the formation of Rainbow Bridge actually make it both a bridge and an arch.

Helmut Friedrich

off-road car. Hiking is prohibited. Monument Valley conveys an impression of magnificent dimensions at all times of the day, intensifying at sunrise and even more at sunset, as well as monumental solemnity. Particularly impressive lookout points are the views of Left and Right Mitten and Merrick Butte right at the park's entrance as well as Artist Point, North Window and Ford's Point. All vehicles must have left the valley by sundown.

A detour worth making on this excursion is one to the *Gooseneck State Reserve*. Some 240 kilometres (150 miles) east of Page are three 180-degree turns of the San Juan River directly following one another, a natural wonder which is probably unique in the world. From a platform 3,000 metres (10,000 feet) high, at the end of the only six kilometre (3.7 mile) long route 316 from Highway 261, the deeply grooved turns can be clearly seen.

Natural Bridges National Monument. This natural monument is a little north of Mexican Hat and can be reached over Highways 95 and 275. The lookout point has a view of the three sandstone bridges discovered in 1883, the largest of which has a span of 81 metres (265 feet) and a height of 67 metres (220 feet); these bridges are connected by a 13-kilometre (8-mile) ring road.

Navajo National Monument. Some 125 kilometres (77 miles) southeast of Page is the Navajo National Monument. Three former Indian settlements, Betatakin, Keet Seel and Inscription House can be visited here. A short path runs from the parking lot to the lookout point, from where one can see the Betatakin Ruins in a gigantic cave. Visiting these or other ruins implies exhausting hikes or rides. Information and registration: Navajo National Monument, HC-71 Box 3, Tonalea, Arizona 86044.

Old Paria Ghost Town. Seventy kilometres (43 miles) west of Page at the end of a northern detour of route 89 is a small ghost town which was reconstructed for a movie: a few wooden houses in front of clay hills with vermilion, brown, white and green layers. Rarely visited.

Caution is advised: the otherwise good access road turns into soft soap when it rains and is no longer passable even on foot or bicycle.

Above: The Owachomo Bridge, one of the three stone bridges of the Natural Bridges National Monument. Below: The narrow bends, Goosenecks, of the San Juan River, a Colorado tributary.

Paria Canyon Trailhead. South of the Page-Kanab route 89, sixty kilometres (37 miles) west of Page, the Paria Canyon Trail begins, a footpath on which runs an exacting multi-day tour – dangerous in stormy weather – to Lee's Ferry on the east end of Grand Canyon National Park. There are unique pink-white sandstone formations at the trailhead.

Zion National Park. Approximately 200 kilometres (125 miles) west of Page is Zion National Park, an area refreshingly green, for it is irrigated by the Virgin River. From the Zion Canyon valley, the heart of the park, attractive walks are possible, such as the one to the *Emerald Pools*. *Weeping Rock* is another destination. Ground water continuously oozes from here, after having spent several years making its way from the high plain to this spot. A footpath runs from the northern end of the canyon into the *Narrows*, an abyss through which the Virgin River flows. The *Hanging Gardens* are worth seeing: ground water allows the growth of succulent plants on the sandstone walls.

The eastern part of the park has a completely different character. Here, at a height of approximately 1,500 metres (5,000 feet), are petrified dunes. The most famous is the *Checkerboard Mesa*.

Above: Along the South Kaibab Trail on the South Rim of the Grand Canyon.
Below: A reconstructed abandoned mining settlement: Old Paria Ghost Town.

LIST OF SOURCES

Bruce Babbitt (comp.), *Grand Canyon – An Anthology*. Flagstaff: Northland Press, 1978
Simone de Beauvoir, *America Day by Day*; Trans. Patrick Dudley. London: Gerald Duckworth & Co. Ltd., 1952. (*L'Amerique au Jour le Jour*. Paris: Editions Paul Morihien, 1950)
John Charles Freemont, *Report on the Exploration of the Country Lying between the Missouri River and the Rocky Mountains*. New York, 1843
Zane Grey, "The Heritage of the Desert", in *Popular Magazine*, 1910
George P. Hammond. Agapito Ray, *Narratives of the Coronado Expedition*. Albuquerque: University of New Mexico Press, 1940
Joseph Wood Krutch, *Grand Canyon, Today and All Its Yesterdays*. New York: Columbia University Press, 1950
John Wesley Powell, *Explorations of the Colorado River of the West and Its Tributaries*. Washington D.C.: Government Printing Office, 1875
Theodore Roosevelt, *A Book Lover's Holiday in the Open*. New York: Charles Scribner's Sons, 1916
Robert Brewster Stanton, "Through the Grand Cañon of the Colorado", in *Scribner's Magazine*, 1890
Wallace Stegner, *The Sound of Mountain Water*. New York: Doubleday & Company, Inc., 1969
Frank Water, *The Colorado*. New York: Rinehart & Co., Inc. 1946

We would like to thank all copyright holders for their kind permission to reprint. Despite intensive efforts on our part, we were not able to contact all copyright holders. Those to whom this applies are asked to contact us.

LIST OF ILLUSTRATIONS

The map on page 48 was drawn by Astrid Fischer-Leitl, Munich.
C.J. Bucher Photo Archive: page 49 top and bottom.
Helmut Friedrich, Möhrendorf: page 38 bottom; page 56 left; page 59 top right and bottom right; page 60 top and bottom; page 61 top; page 62 top and bottom; page 63 top and bottom; page 64.
All other photographs by Christian Heeb.

DESTINATION GRAND CANYON
WINDSOR BOOKS INTERNATIONAL, 1993

© English Text by Verlag C.J. Bucher GmbH, Munich 1993

Translation: Naomi Sidaway Sollinger
Editor: Karen Lemiski
Anthology: Karen Lemiski